Annette Black
Michael B. Barry
Introduction by Michael Phillips

BRIDGES OF DUBLIN
THE REMARKABLE STORY OF DUBLIN'S LIFFEY BRIDGES

Dublin City Council

Comhairle Cathrach
Bhaile Átha Cliath
Dublin City Council

Published by Dublin City Council
Civic Offices
Wood Quay
Dublin D08 RF3F
www.dublincity.ie

Hardback edition: ISBN 978-1-907002-25-0
Paperback edition: ISBN 978-1-907002-21-2

Dublin City Council © 2015

Jacket design by Anú Design
Book design by Michael B. Barry

Printed by Print Media Services, Dublin.

ACKNOWLEDGEMENTS

Dublin City Council contributors: the concept of this book was originated by Michael Phillips, City Engineer, whose inspirational paper on Dublin's bridges was the basis for much of the text of this book. Images were curated by Anthony Mc Guinness and Peter Dee, supported by Mary Clarke of the Dublin City Library & Archive. Maps of the individual bridges were provided by Thomas Curran. The production of the book was project managed by Dermot Kinane and Grainne McDermott. Many thanks are due to all for their diligent and dedicated work.

   Warm thanks are also due to: Liam Meagher, Ken Wade, Michael Kiernan and Joe Walsh of Iarnród Éireann, also the staff at the archives of Engineers Ireland.

www.bridgesofdublin.ie

CONTENTS

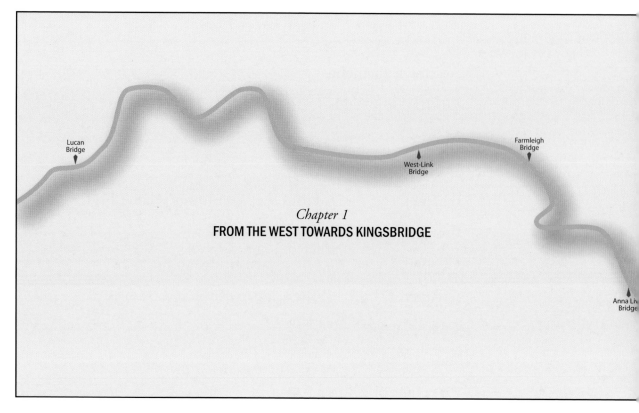

Chapter 1
FROM THE WEST TOWARDS KINGSBRIDGE

(Map labels: Lucan Bridge; West-Link Bridge; Farmleigh Bridge; Anna Livia Bridge)

ILLUSTRATION CREDITS

Images on the specified pages are courtesy of the following (abbreviations for top, bottom, left, middle, right, respectively, are: t, b, l, m, r):

Airman Jason Byrne, Defence Forces of Ireland: 216t. Anthony Mc Guinness: 220t. Dermot O'Dwyer, TCD: 56t. Donal Murphy Photography: 10-11; 16-17t; 34-35; 57; 58-59; 130-131; 138-139; 148-149; 155b; 177t; 190-191; 196-197; 204-205; 234-235. Dublin City Library & Archive: 5b; 33t; 38t; 39t; 39bl; 40t; 40br; 47bl; 60br; 72t; 74br; 75t; 75m; 82br; 84-85; 89bl; 92t; 93t; 100-101t; 107t; 110-111; 128tr; 129t; 129bl; 134-135; 136t; 143; 144br; 146t; 146tr; 154t; 154b; 161bl; 164t; 164br; 166t; 166br; 168t; 168b; 169t; 174t; 174b; 192t; 193bl; 194t; 194br; 195t; 208t; 209t; 209b; 210t; 211b; 213t; 223t; 226-227t; 230b; 233br; 237t; images on pages 240-251 (except 240b & 250t). Dublin Port Company: 153b. Fáilte Ireland: 119t; 144m. Flickr user Roantrum: 141bl. Guinness Archive, Diageo Ireland: 82t; 98t; 118t. Iarnród Éireann: 53bl; 54t; 55t; 184t; 185t; 187t; 189t; 230t; 250t. Irish Architectural Archive: 55br; 153t; 230m; 233bl. Irish Capuchin Provincial Archives: 105bl; 112br. Irish Photographic Archive: 128br. Irish Times: 137t (Dara Mac Dónaill); 201b (Bryan O'Brien); 219t (Cyril Byrne). Jason Clarke Photography: 50-51; 76-77; 88-89t; 92t; 94-95; 102-103; 106br; 118br; 120-121; 136br; 170-171; 216br; 238br; 239tl; 239ml. John Burke: 42-43. Joseph McGarrity Collection, Digital Library@Villanova University: 158b; 233ml. Kilmainham Gaol Archives: 100br (KMGLM 2015.0581). Mary Croke Photography: 20b; 22t; 25t; 60t; 70t; 73t; 74t; 75bl; 214-215; 218t; 218m; 236t. Michael B. Barry: 4-5t map; 17B; 30; 31t; 41t; 54br; 64t; 64br (Photografx); 65; 66t; 67t; 68-69; 80b; 81bl; 83t; 86br; 90br; 92bl; 99bl; 99t; 108; 127bl; 128l; 140br; 145; 155t; 160; 161t; 178-179; 180-181; 185b; 186t; 188; 200t; 202t; 203t; 211t; 212t; 212br; 222br; 223bl; 224tr; 224br; 225tl; all images on 238 except br; all images on 239 except tl and mr; 238bl map; 239br map. National Gallery of Ireland: 14-15; 44-45t; 106t; 114-115; 116t; 124-125; 158t; 159t; 221t; 231. National Library of Ireland: 38b; 46br; 48-49t; 62-63; 66b; 79bl; 109t; 117t; 126t; 142t; 152t; 157bl; 159b; 175t; 176t; 183t; 187b; 228-229; 233t. National Maritime Museum of Ireland: 233mr. National Transport Museum of Ireland: 201t. Oliver Hickey: 26-27; 32t; 32b. Peter Barrow Photography: 12t; 20t; 28t; 36t; 46t; 52t; 78t; 86t; 96t; 104t; 112t; 122t; 132t; 140t; 150t; 172t; 198t; 206t; 208m. Ron Cox, Engineers Ireland: 174br. Royal Society of Antiquaries Ireland: 80t; 122br. Santiago Calatrava LLC: 87bl; 90t; 91t; 91bl; 91br. South Dublin County Council: 13. Thomas Fitzgerald Photography: 162-163; 167t. Transport Infrastructure Ireland: 18-19; 23t; 24; 67tl; 240b. Wikimedia Commons/Mutter Erde: 45bl.

Ordnance Survey Ireland ©, maps on pages: 13t; 21t; 29t; 37t; 47t; 53t; 61t; 71t; 79t; 87t; 97t; 105t; 113t; 123t; 133t; 141t; 151t; 165t; 173t; 182t; 193t; 199t; 207t; 217t. Every effort has been made to establish copyright, but if a copyright holder wishes to bring an error to the notice of the publishers, then an appropriate acknowledgement will be made in any subsequent edition.

Above: a schematic of the present-day bridges of Dublin, along the Liffey, from Lucan to the sea.

4

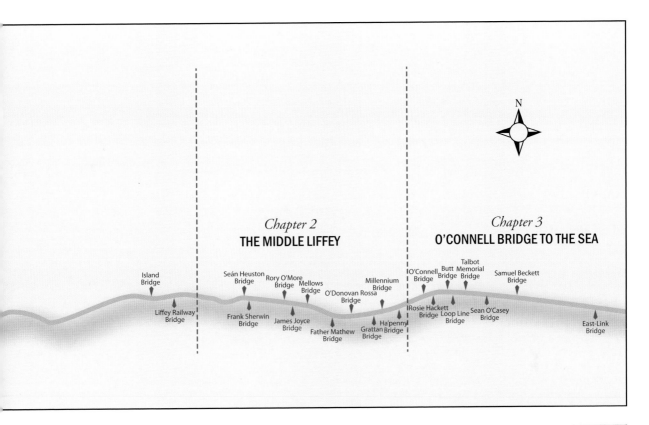

Chapter 2
THE MIDDLE LIFFEY

Chapter 3
O'CONNELL BRIDGE TO THE SEA

Island Bridge

Liffey Railway Bridge

Seán Heuston Bridge

Rory O'More Bridge

Mellows Bridge

O'Donovan Rossa Bridge

Millennium Bridge

Frank Sherwin Bridge

James Joyce Bridge

Father Mathew Bridge

Grattan Bridge

Ha'penny Bridge

O'Connell Bridge

Rosie Hackett Bridge

Butt Bridge

Loop Line Bridge

Talbot Memorial Bridge

Sean O'Casey Bridge

Samuel Beckett Bridge

East-Link Bridge

Right: John Speed's map of Dublin, in 1610. Only one bridge crossed the Liffey at that time. It was on the site of the present-day Father Mathew Bridge, and is listed on the map as, logically enough: 'The Bridge'.

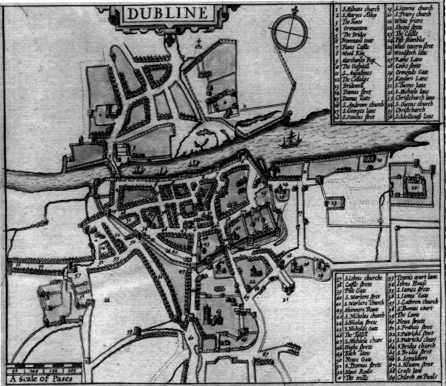

INTRODUCTION

The meaning of the word 'bridge' has been interpreted in many ways but overall it reflects the bringing together and the connection of people and communities. It is not known when man first understood the relevance of building a structure to cross a river but, by the Stone Age man began to use tools. At this time, a primitive understanding of adapting timber and stone to serve a community's needs emerged. And these were the two main materials used for bridges until the 19th century.

Wood has been used as far back as the Neolithic era to cross rivers. It is estimated that 17,000 years ago, covered logs, laid flat, were used for the first wooden bridges. The first documented accounts of wooden bridges are from 2,000 to 3,000 years ago, and were used for crossing the Euphrates and certain tributaries of the Nile.

However, it wasn't until the height of the Roman Empire (circa 100 BC) that more advanced timber bridges, in particular those with beams, strut frames and arches, were developed. Caesar's bridge across the Rhine, where the width of the river was 140 metres, was built in only 10 days and is an excellent example of timber bridges in those times – they were simple, generally temporary in nature and were frequently washed away by floodwaters.

In medieval times, timber bridges became common and had become more complex. Timber deck bridges built then generally used stone piers on timber pile foundations. Rot was wood's major enemy – an average lifespan for timber bridges was approximately 25 years. Over time, timber bridges went out of favour and were generally only used as temporary structures or where economic conditions would not allow for more permanent solutions in stone.

Timber bridges got a new lease of life in the 18th and 19th centuries, particularly in the USA where it is estimated that approximately 10,000 timber bridges were built between 1805 and 1885. This revival can be attributed to a number of factors including: the development of creosote; the transfer of knowledge from the new European settlers and the fact that timber as a lightweight material was ideally suited for use in the newly developed technique of suspension bridges. Many covered bridges and bridges with spans up to 85 metres were built during this period. Several remain in service today. However, for longer spans, timber simply did not provide sufficient strength for the heavier loads for which bridges were being designed during the great age of railway construction.

More recently during the 20th century, there has been a renewed interest in timber as a bridge building material, particularly for footbridges. Developments in the use of timber in bridge construction include the design of decks from pre-stressed wood and the use of glued-laminated wood.

Stone bridges have been used in one form or another for many thousands of years. The earliest surviving stone structures are clapper bridges. These are an elementary form of stone bridge formed by large flat slabs of stone. The use of the arch was important in the development of bridges. The oldest surviving record of the use of the arch shape as a structural form is the Arkadiko Bridge, dating to the 13th century BC, which is one of four Mycenaean stone corbel-arch bridges that form part of an ancient network of roads, designed to accommodate chariots in Greece.

In the very early years of bridge construction the use of bricks was very rare, although brick-built bridges with carriageways supported on vaults were constructed in Mesopotamia from at least the 6th century BC. However, it was the Romans who were the greatest masonry bridge builders of antiquity. They had a great understanding of forces, geometry and the properties of stone and this allowed them to create spans significantly greater than anything that the world had seen before. The genius of the Roman bridge builders can be seen with the six-span bridge over the river Tagus at Alcantra in Spain, which contains individual spans of up to 30 metres and the Pont du Gard in Southern France where the lower levels of arches have no cement in the joints.

At about the same time the Chinese were also developing bridges with new geometries (segmental, elliptical, parabolic, etc.). The Zhaozhou Bridge, built around 600 AD during the Sui Dynasty, in China is historically significant as it is the world's oldest open-spandrel, stone, segmental-arch bridge.

After the decline of the Roman Empire, stone bridges continued to be constructed but not in large numbers. They were expensive as they required a large number of skilled labourers and took many years to build. Thus, large stone bridges were more often constructed under the influence of the Christian Church throughout the middle ages and the Renaissance period. For many of these bridges no expense was spared in overcoming some of the most difficult obstacles as it was seen as glorifying God in much the same way as the construction of cathedrals. The Charles Bridge in Prague is a typical example where the bridge itself almost became a site of religious pilgrimage.

In terms of volume, the main period of sustained masonry arch building began with the development of the canal systems in the second half of the 18th century and continued with the construction of the railway systems throughout the 19th century. During this period many tens of thousands of masonry-arch bridges were built, the vast majority of which remain in service today. However, the completion of the boom in railway construction spelled the end of the use of stone and brick in bridge construction. Very few of these have been built since.

A major breakthrough in bridge technology came with the erection of the Iron Bridge, over the River Severn, near Coalbrookdale, England in 1779. Here, for the first time, cast iron was used for the arches of a bridge. Until 1840 the construction material used was either cast iron or wrought iron or a combination of both. In the early 1800s cast iron began to be replaced by wrought iron and many of the early railway bridges were built of wrought-iron construction. During the 19th century, lattice-truss systems composed of wrought iron were developed for larger span bridges. However, iron did not have the tensile strength to support very large loads. Later in the century, the advent of steel, which has a high tensile strength, allowed the construction of much longer span bridges.

Concrete has been used in construction for over 2,000 years when it was widely used by the Chinese and the Romans. Examples include the dome of the Pantheon in Rome, also nearly 5,600 km of Roman roads were mainly made up of concrete material. However, with the fall of the Roman Empire the use of concrete largely disappeared for nearly 13 centuries until a method for producing Portland cement was patented in 1824. This was quickly followed in 1849 when Joseph Monier combined metal with concrete to create reinforced concrete. Since then, it has become the major construction material for bridges, as it has for most structural and civil engineering applications. This is due to its intrinsic versatility, design, flexibility and above all, natural durability.

Over the second half of the 19th century, concrete bridges were almost entirely arch structures as this produced compression, rather than tensile forces. Concrete was simply poured into timber formwork to create monolithic structures quickly and cheaply. However, the problems with this new material soon became apparent as it was noted that it could easily crack due to differential movement.

In the first decade of the 20th century steel reinforcement, as we know it today, was introduced and allowed for more diverse geometries to be developed as well as the capacity to cater for tensile forces. During this time, much of the large scale use of reinforced concrete was pioneered by the French builder Francois Hennebique. It was at around this time too that the use of precast concrete was developed for the first time. The original Mizen Head footbridge, built in 1908 in West Cork, was an outstanding example of one of the first precast reinforced concrete structures. Over nearly 30 years the use of reinforced concrete developed rapidly worldwide. During the following decades the next advance for concrete bridges was the advent of prestressed concrete, as developed by Eugene Freyissinet. This allowed for very large-span and economical concrete structures to be constructed. The expansion of the motorway network in Europe during the latter half of the 20th century resulted in large numbers of concrete bridges being built.

During the 1970s and 1980s, the Swiss Federal Laboratories for Materials Research undertook research in the area of the strengthening of reinforced concrete bridges using glass, carbon and aramid fibre-reinforced polymers. Polymers have many advantages: lightness, high strength, durability and corrosion resistance. In 1992, the Aberfeldy footbridge over the River Tay in Scotland was the world's first major advanced composite bridge. The Bonds Mill Lifting Bridge in Surrey of 1995 was the first entirely fibre-reinforced polymer road bridge. Hundreds more bridges containing fibre-reinforced polymer components such as decks, beams, trusses, rebar, tendons, or panels have been constructed over the last 20 years. However, there are several issues that are still being researched, including; uncertainties in relation to long term performance; higher initial costs and lack of nationally accepted standards. As solutions are found there is no doubt that this will continue to be an area of extremely rapid growth in the future.

From the most advanced bridge technology, we now look back in time to the simplest form of crossing a river: a ford. During the first millennium, the Liffey in Dublin was initially crossed by three fords. Two of these fords were located close to where the river bed was exposed at low water, located between the present-day Four Courts and Capel Street. The third ford was situated at Island Bridge.

When the Vikings came to Dublin and settled, things became more sophisticated. There are accounts that they built a timber bridge across the river, near their mud and wattle settlement. Viking timber longships are well built, able to withstand long voyages through Atlantic storms. They brought this boat-building skill to the banks of the Liffey, as evidenced by the exquisite longboat that they made in Dublin (a replica of which was on display at the National Museum of Ireland some years ago). If they applied some of this skill in the building of Dublin's first bridge, it must have been a substantial and fine structure. It was the Normans, masters of stone fortification who built the first stone bridge in Dublin.

The city, then tiny, marked time somewhat over the rest of the medieval era. From earliest times through the medieval period, there is little written about the bridges of Dublin. Prior to the arrival of James Butler, 1st Duke of Ormonde mentions are made of structures beyond the city limits at Kilmainham, Chapelizod and Lucan. The city itself had only one bridge in 1610 but by 1673 when de Gomme drew his map of the city of Dublin there were two. The energy and drive of James Butler heralded a period of expansion for the city ultimately leading to many initiatives such as the Phoenix Park, the Royal Hospital at Kilmainham and the Royal (now Collins) Barracks (then the largest barracks in the world). The underlying reason for these may have been for the better control of Dublin or for the enjoyment of the small ruling coterie. However, these are among the principal sights and buildings that underpin Dublin as a European capital today. In turn as the city developed, so did the number of bridges: by around 1700 three new and two replacement bridges had been built.

Architectural treasures of Georgian Dublin (1714-1830) include the simple but elegant Ha'penny Bridge and the distinctive King's Bridge. It was during this time too that Gandon built the Carlisle Bridge where O'Connell Bridge now stands. Rebuilds too took place from far flung Lucan and Chapelizod, to emerging suburbs at Island Bridge as well as in the heart of the city itself.

Industry and commerce dictated the pace and style of much of the bridge building of the 19th century: railway bridges were the Liffey Railway Bridge and the controversial Loop Line Bridge (both of latticed truss type); O'Connell Bridge was rebuilt to a wider design to accommodate traffic; iron, the new building material of the industrial revolution, was again used on the Victoria and Albert (Rory O'More) and Essex (Grattan) Bridges. A metal swivel section was incorporated into the city's most easterly new crossing, Butt Bridge and the Guinness family built their own wrought-iron bridge to bring piped water and electric power to their grand mansion at Farmleigh. Butt Bridge was rebuilt in 1932 but it was not until 1978 when there was a new bridge across the river – the Talbot Memorial Bridge. After this, and in parallel with a significant period of economic growth (interspersed with some significant recessions) there has been a surge in the number of Liffey bridges in Dublin – we have now reached a total of 24.

Dublin has experienced every type of bridge over the Liffey: timber (long departed); masonry; cast iron; wrought iron; steel; reinforced concrete and pre-stressed and post-tensioned concrete. In structural form, the range is wide, from masonry arch, all the way to the cable stays of the Samuel Beckett Bridge.

Equally eclectic is the range of bridge names which arose from our tangled history. Originally the names were unfailingly royal, mostly those of our viceregal or ducal rulers. Newly independent countries tend to change names of public places such as bridges and streets, as part of a collective shedding of traces of the oppression of the previous order. Thus it was for the Dublin bridges. All the colonial-era names were changed, particularly during the first half of the 20th century. Maybe it reflects calmer political times, but now we are able to focus more on social and literary issues than specifically the struggle for independence. Recent bridges have been named after three outstanding literary figures, all closely associated with Dublin – it also reflects the recognition of Dublin as a city of culture. The naming of the newest bridge after Rosie Hackett is also a sea change – to name a bridge after a woman who struggled for women's rights, as well as being a veteran of 1916.

This book presents the story of the 24 bridges that span the Liffey, within Dublin city and county. The bridges have been divided up into chapters. Chapter One includes those western bridges along the river – those in a more rural, out-of-town setting. Chapter Two includes the historic bridges (including the oldest) in the heart of the city. With two exceptions, all the bridges here date from the Georgian and Victorian eras. Chapter Three starts with O'Connell Bridge, a Victorian bridge built upon Gandon's Georgian one. The newest bridge, the Rosie Hackett, is followed by three functional bridges in concrete and latticed steel. Two new bridges of outstanding design follow: the Sean O'Casey and the Samuel Beckett. Our journey ends on a muted note at the edge of the bay: the workaday East-Link Bridge.

Care was taken to include maps showing the location of each bridge. This to help people who wish to go and see the bridges – which I encourage. This collection of bridges along the Liffey is an essential part of our heritage and is worth seeing for a host of reasons: aesthetic, historical and even from an engineering point-of-view. On pages 238 and 239, two convenient routes for a tour are shown: a walk west up the Liffey from the Ha'penny Bridge; the other is to walk downriver from O'Connell Bridge to the East-Link. On each of these, you can see a mix of bridges, from the ancient and historical, to the sparkling new. At the end of the book, just in case you are suffering from technical indigestion, or a surfeit of acronyms, there is a glossary. And for those of you who are technical, we have included drawings of the bridges as a finale to the book.

The website *www.bridgesofdublin.ie* was one of the inspirations for this book. Much of the information and images were sourced from that prepared for the website. It is very much worthwhile visiting this – it contains a wealth of further information on Dublin's bridges.

The story of Dublin's bridges, now over a thousand years, is a continuing one. Things change as the city develops. As I write, two additional pedestrian walkways are planned for the Liffey. Another road bridge, in the area where the Grand Canal and River Dodder meet the Liffey, is also being commissioned. This book is a snap-shot of the bridges of the Liffey in 2015. I hope, you, dear reader, experience the same enjoyment of this unique part of our heritage, as I have done over a good part of my career, of building and maintaining these bridges.

Michael Phillips
City Engineer, Dublin
September 2015

Chapter 1
FROM THE WEST TOWARDS KINGSBRIDGE
ANIAR I dTREO KINGSBRIDGE

A print of Island Bridge, dating from 1820

As the Liffey flows from the Wicklow Mountains towards the sea, the population density increases as it comes closer to Dublin. In turn the network of roads increases. We start this chapter with a historic bridge at Lucan, still the longest-span masonry arch bridge in Ireland. In our journey along the river, we next encounter road bridges, old and new. Finally we reach the Liffey Railway Bridge, a 19th-century bridge built to carry the railway over the river, then through a tunnel under the Phoenix Park, which then loops round the city to reach the docks.

LUCAN BRIDGE

DROICHEAD LEAMHCÁIN

CROSSES FROM LOWER ROAD TO LOWER LUCAN ROAD

ROAD BRIDGE   MASONRY ARCH   1813

L ucan Bridge, located in the busy town of the same name, crosses from the Lower Road to the Lower Lucan Road and is some 13 kilometres from Dublin city centre. When constructed it was, at 34 metres, the longest single arch masonry bridge in Ireland, a record it still holds.

George Knowles, the designer, drew inspiration from the Island Bridge downriver – itself favourably compared to Venice's Rialto Bridge. Previously he had worked on the design of the O'Donovan Rossa Bridge of 1816 and the Father Mathew Bridge, completed in 1818. Their costs, at £25,950 and £26,000 respectively, were far greater than the £9,000 recorded as being the final expenditure for Lucan Bridge. Even so, Knowles was accused of an intentional cost overrun in pursuit of the longest-span record as the geology of the river would have allowed for a bridge with a shorter span.

The walls of Lucan Bridge are of squared limestone, with the distinctive black hue of locally quarried stone. Slender voussoirs or wedge-shaped stones form the curve of the single, segmental arch of the bridge. The initial design proposed that the parapet too should be of stone but this was changed to more elegant cast-iron balusters made by the Royal Phoenix Ironworks of Parkgate Street in Dublin, where later the cast-iron King's (now Seán Heuston) Bridge was manufactured. Mellows Bridge of 1768 had a similar balus-

Above: Lucan Bridge, as elegant as it was when built. It may be over two centuries old, but it still carries modern road traffic over the Liffey.

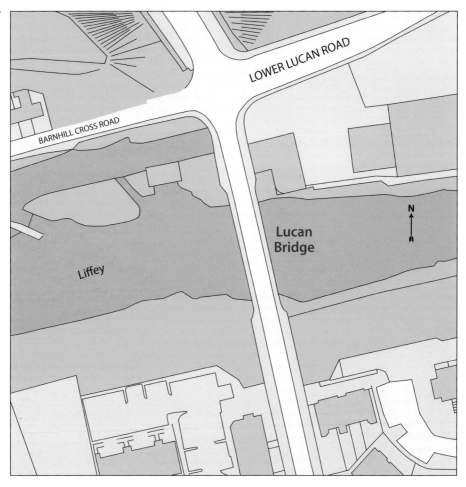

trade added during a refurbishment in 1818 whilst both O'Donovan Rossa Bridge and Father Mathew Bridge are also embellished with cast-iron balusters.

Records tell us that construction of the great arch of the bridge began in April 1813, an event notable enough to be reported in the press. A Mrs Vesey laid the keystone in November 1813. It was also reported that the bridge was open to traffic in 1813. A traffic accident shortly after inflicted no damage to the bridge structure. The date 1814 is recorded on the bridge parapet, probably the final completion date – indicating that the bridge may have been in use for some time with a temporary parapet.

A bridge has existed here from as far back as the reign of King John in the 13th century – the same monarch who sanctioned the city's first stone bridge where today Father Mathew Bridge stands. The structure here was on the lands of one Alex Fitzwilliam who had charge of the gallows, the hunting of the stags and other interests of the king. As this was a strategic location, it was most likely a sturdy stone bridge as favoured by the Normans. In the late 15th century, during the reign of Henry VI, two watch towers were added to the bridge at Lucan – Henry was mindful of the danger of enemies attacking from the west. Records of 1663 tell of 'a good stone bridge' at Lucan and in

1714 of the 'great road west over the Lucan Bridge'. Undoubtedly undocumented repairs and rebuilds took place as bridges along the Liffey frequently fell to floods. Bridges were poorly constructed or, due to the parsimony of the public purse, badly maintained.

The pretty, pastoral location of Lucan Bridge attracted amateur and professional painters. Mary Delany, (friend of Jonathan Swift, the composer Handel and Queen Charlotte, wife of George III) depicted a stone bridge in her painting of 1749. The view is partially obscured with only three arches visible. Thomas Roberts' painting of around 1773 shows a masonry bridge of at least five arches with an uneven parapet. In the foreground workmen quarry stone – quite possibly for repair of the bridge.

Above: pretty and pastoral. Thomas Roberts' painting from around 1773 shows a stone-arched bridge at Lucan.

Lucan was also a popular place of retreat for affluent Dubliners and day trippers alike since the medicinal qualities of its spa had been discovered around 1758. The journey from the city, along the Lower Road and across the Lucan Bridge was a delight in itself. High wooded slopes loomed on either side with elm, oak and ash shading the road. At the bottom of the valley the Liffey ran along, here and there broken by a mill weir which produced cascades of water. In places, the river, with large stone boulders arrayed along, was shallow enough to cross.

Lucan Bridge was a busy one – on one summer day in 1794 thousands of pedestrians, 55 coaches, 29 post chaises, 25 noddies, 82 jaunting cars, 20 gigs, six open landaus, 221 common cars and 450 horsemen were recorded as having crossed here.

In 1802 it was reported that the bridge had been destroyed by floods. In 1805 a 'permanent' wooden bridge was erected. It was repaired again following floods in 1807. A serious accident occurred in March 1811 when a turf-laden cart owned by Messrs Guinness crashed through the parapets of the wooden bridge and plunged into the Liffey. Following this, influential voices were raised advocating the need for a new bridge. They argued that the 'heavy tax' paid by bridge users and the very danger presented to their lives by poor quality repairs and rebuilds justified the expense. It seems the bridge at Lucan, in common with other bridges and roads, was at that time, tolled.

Lucan Bridge, or the Liffey Bridge at Lucan as it is sometimes known, is named for the local area. *Leamhán* is an Irish term for elm and *cán* denotes 'place'. Lucan is from an anglicised form of *Leamh-cán*. Patrick Sarsfield was the first Earl of Lucan – his family were landowners in the area from the late 1500s. Patrick was born around 1650 to Anne, daughter of the rebel nobleman Rory O'More for whom another Liffey bridge is named. Indeed, Seán Heuston Bridge was known as Sarsfield Bridge from 1922 to 1941.

Lucan Bridge today is just as it was in 1813 though the approach gradient was reduced as the vertical sighting distance was unsafe for modern traffic. In 2011 the stonework was repointed, capstones replaced and the balustrades given a fresh coat of paint.

Simply elegant, Lucan Bridge – a Liffey treasure.

Above: the span, graceful over the river. The design drew inspiration from Island Bridge.

Below: the cast-iron balustrades make a fine curved pattern over the arch.

The Structure

Lucan Bridge is a single-span, segmental arch structure. At 34 metres in length it is the longest masonry arch bridge in Ireland. It carries vehicular and pedestrian traffic. The bridge material is limestone, squared, and, of all the Liffey bridges, it is generally considered one of the finer examples of ashlar masonry.

The arch curve is drawn in ashlar voussoirs, the arch itself having the distinctive black hue of local stone and its crest is marked by a decorative keystone. The skewback, resting on an impost, is formed of three stones, with a springing face at 45 degrees to the horizontal. Solid, 1.8 metre-thick pier abutments back the springings on each side as far as road level. In addition the springing commences less than a metre above rock level so it is well founded and horizontal movement is restricted. The bridge rise is 6.7 metres. The balustrades are of cast iron, resting on a stone plinth and laid in series with interspacing dadoes, all of the same size.

Designed by George Knowles, this bridge of 1813 cost £9,000.

WEST-LINK BRIDGE
DROICHEAD AN NASCBHÓTHAIR THIAR
CROSSES THE LIFFEY VALLEY
ROAD BRIDGE   CONCRETE   1990

The Liffey curves gently through an irregular patchwork of trimmed green fields at the Strawberry Beds, set in a deep, beautiful valley a mere stone's throw from Dublin city centre. A place of culinary pilgrimage through much of the 18th and well into the 19th centuries, Dubliners trekked here, by foot, carriage and omnibus, just to savour the heavenly strawberries which grew abundantly on the sunny terraces stepping back from the river's north bank.

In those days the river was lazy and languid as it flowed through the valley, reflected pleasing summer scenes of lady artists in wide-brimmed hats, gentlemen poets and pedlars offering cupped lettuce leaves brimming with dappled berries and a splash of thick, sweet cream from a cold earthenware jug. There was, until 1787, a charming wooden bridge here too, constructed by Lord Carhampton of nearby Luttrellstown. Honeymooners favoured the valley and its romantic lure lasted well into the 20th century when the Dubliners folk band sang in 'The Ferryman':

Where the Strawberry Beds sweep down to the Liffey
You kiss away the worries from my brow

Today a large concrete structure is reflected, perhaps incongruously, in those same waters – the West-Link Bridge. In January 1988, construction of the bridge began. Into the quietness of this hidden valley giant earthmovers rumbled and deep excavations were made in the patchwork of fields running down to the river. Hollow, geometric pillars of concrete rose skywards from which, in due course, each section of the giant bridge deck was constructed in situ and cantilevered out from specially constructed pier supports – to the un-

Above: a line of grey cuts through the sylvan green. West-Link Bridge from the air.

Below: deep foundations reaching to bedrock. Construction started in 1988.

Right: map of the West-Link Bridge. It carries four lanes of the M50 Motorway in each direction across the deep valley of the Liffey at the Strawberry Beds.

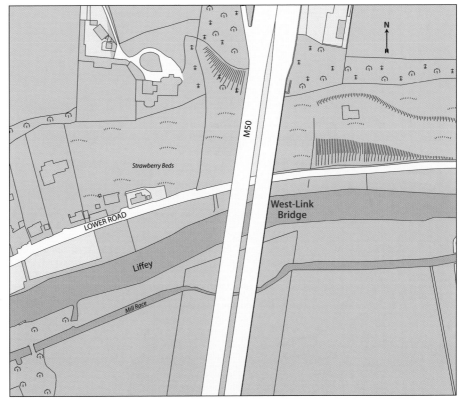

tutored eye seemingly precariously, projecting into the horizontal space above the valley, until eventually meeting the next bridge deck in mid span. Those gazing skywards from the valley below spied miniature, helmeted construction workers hammering and drilling amidst what looked like an industrial landscape shelved between earth and sky.

There is nothing romantic about this workaday bridge, the West-Link. It has little architectural merit, though it can boast of some impressive statistics. It is the most elevated of the Liffey bridges, reaching a maximum height of 42 metres above the river. It is of five spans, one of 90 metres, and its overall length is 385 metres. The West-Link is, in fact, two independent bridges – the original bridge of 1990, which now carries northbound traffic, and the newer addition, a duplicate of the first bridge, which opened in 2003, carries southbound traffic. It was the first new bridge built west of the city boundary in over 100 years as 20th-century sprawl swallowed up the country villages to the west of Dublin city which had, up to then, mainly developed along a west-to-east axis.

The genesis of the West-Link Bridge is in the 1971 Dublin Transportation Study which recommended a 360-degree circuit road for Dublin and envisaged a completion date of 1991. Including the Port Tunnel, a 300-degree loop has been achieved, the controversial Eastern Bypass never having been built. Given limited central and local government capacity for such expensive projects, the 1979 Local Government (Toll Roads) Act was a necessary step to encourage private sector investment in public infrastructure projects. In

1987 final agreement was reached with the West Link Toll Bridge Ltd (owned by National Toll Roads) and Dublin County Council for the construction and operation of what was designated the West-Link Toll Bridge. During the design process, a topographical model of the Liffey Valley was made and used to examine the impact of a bridge, and the possibility of a second, on the area. Scale models were used to examine the aesthetics of the piers and deck in relation to the valley. Construction, by Irishenco, began in January 1988 to a design by Ove Arup and Partners.

The bridge was declared open on the 11th March 1990 by Taoiseach Charles Haughey. Then a mere two-lane bridge, one lane northbound and the other southbound, it was part of the 12.2 km Western Parkway Motorway. The West-Link Toll Bridge Ltd was responsible for 3.2 km of that motorway which included the bridge and linked the N3 Navan road with the N4 Lucan route. The state funded the remaining nine km section. Costing a reported €35 million (including land costs), it was then the most expensive road project undertaken in Ireland. For each crossing the motorist initially paid 60 pence, the Irish pound then being the currency, (equivalent to 76 cent today). Tolls accrued to National Toll Roads though the state coffers benefitted through rates, licence fee, VAT and a revenue sharing agreement.

From the late 1990s the expansion of Dublin, the piecemeal completion of the M50, the rise in car ownership, economic growth and the resultant increase in employment meant the bridge functioned not just as planned –

to divert provincial traffic from Dublin city centre – but as a busy and often congested connector route for Dublin suburban traffic. In September 2001 when VAT was added to the toll price, a supplemental agreement allowed for the building of a second bridge. Construction began and this opened in September 2003 allowing the lane numbers to increase to three in each direction. Later, heavy shields were added to the parapets to allow the bridge to remain open in periods of high winds.

As part of the initial design the West-Link Bridge toll plaza was located at the north end of the bridge and the majority of bridge users paid cash at the booths provided. Long traffic queues, particularly at peak times, were part of daily life for many a harried motorist. Complaints regularly filled newspaper columns and were the subject of much debate over the airwaves. A pre-payment option was added in the early 2000s but did little to relieve the long waiting times at the barriers.

Those legendary jams finally became a thing of the past at the end of August 2008, when barrier-free tolling, which employs electronic licence plate reading technology, was introduced. On the same date, the bridge was formally handed over to the National Roads Authority (NRA), the state body responsible for the national road network. Bridge users now pay the toll by means of a barrier-free electronic toll system operated by eFlow on behalf of the NRA.

This is one of only four Liffey bridges inaccessible to pedestrians (the others being Farmleigh Bridge, currently out of commission, the Liffey Railway Bridge and the Loop Line Bridge). However, in the days before the official opening in 1990, pedestrians were permitted to traverse the new bridge and admire the valley below.

Right: the concrete rises as a pier is constructed. At its highest, the bridge towers 42 metres over the river. There are five spans of pre-stressed concrete box girders, the longest span being 90 metres.

Left: towering over the Liffey Valley. The West-Link Bridge is now made up of two identical bridges. As traffic demand had ramped up, the original bridge (with two lanes in each direction), dating from 1990, had become a bottleneck. A second bridge was constructed alongside, which opened in 2003. Barrier-free electronic tolling was introduced in 2008, which further reduced the bottleneck.

The Structure

The West-Link Toll Bridge is in fact two identical bridges. The first, opened in 1990, carried both north and south bound traffic and was built by Irishenco to a design by Ove Arup and Partners at a cost of around £4.5 million. The second bridge, opened in 2003, now carries southbound traffic with the original structure catering for northbound vehicles. Each bridge is of four lanes and is of a pre-stressed concrete box girder construction of five spans, the longest being 90 metres. The deck was cantilevered out using the balanced cantilever method from special sections at the top of each pier. The box is of a constant depth single cell. At its highest, the West-Link reaches 42 metres above the Liffey, the highest of the bridges over the river, and is 385 metres in length and each of the two bridges is 16.2 metres wide. Since initial construction heavy shields have been added to the parapets of the bridge to allow it to remain open at times of high winds.

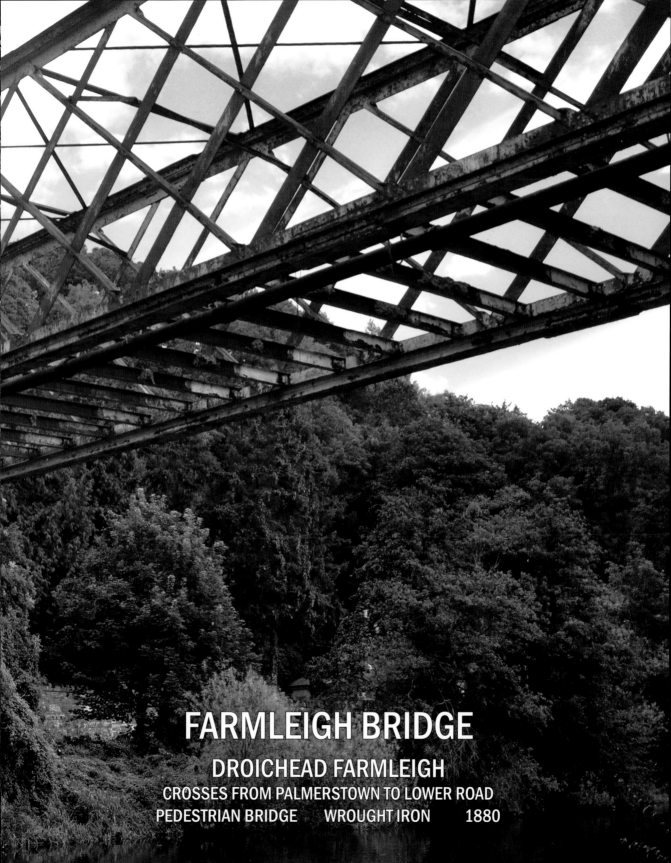

FARMLEIGH BRIDGE

DROICHEAD FARMLEIGH

CROSSES FROM PALMERSTOWN TO LOWER ROAD

PEDESTRIAN BRIDGE　　WROUGHT IRON　　1880

Above: set in a verdant landscape, this lattice truss bridge provided a connection from the Farmleigh Estate to the fields of Palmerstown to the south.

Farmleigh Bridge stretches across the Liffey as a single wrought-iron span of around 52 metres, the lattice girder structure resting on rock-faced, cut limestone abutments. It connects the southern fields of Palmerstown to the Farmleigh Estate in the north-west corner of the Phoenix Park. Once a ford existed here, last recorded in 1773, and all around are remnants of yesteryear – wild flowers, overgrown cottage gardens and tumble-down walls.

The tale of Farmleigh Bridge brings together an improbable trio: romance, industry and inventiveness. In 1872, the Farmleigh house and estate, described by auctioneer Mr McQuestion as the "perfect fairy land" was sold to the young, wealthy and soon-to-be married Edward Cecil Guinness, one of the heirs to the brewing fortune. Later enobled as the first Earl of Iveagh, he was a noted philanthropist, responsible for many generous initiatives in Dublin including public housing near St Patrick's Cathedral.

With a commanding position on the north bank of the Liffey, and adjacent to the Phoenix Park, the house stood amid pleasant meadows, shady copses and exotic gardens with vineries, orchid and azalea houses, fish ponds, fountains, grottoes, croquet lawns and cricket grounds.

Edward Cecil's wife, vivacious and charming Adelaide Maria, a doyenne of the French court, put Farmleigh at the centre of the most elite Dublin social circles. She had married against her mother's wishes – Edward Cecil, though a third cousin, was then a mere commoner and Adelaide had been raised and groomed for the ultimate reward of marriage to an aristocrat. With their ever-increasing riches – Edward Cecil was to become Ireland's richest man in 1886 – the Guinnesses ordered a major refurbishment and building programme for the house around 1880 and to include the 'must have' accessory of the day

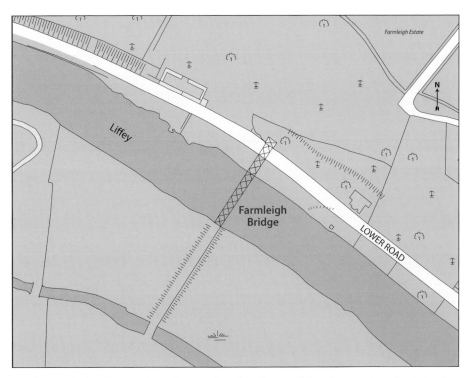

— electric light. It was the advanced technology of the time – the physicist Joseph Swan had given the first public demonstration of his incandescent light bulb a mere two years earlier.

Using the great resources of the Guinness Brewery (then the largest in the world) work began on improvements to the estate. Included in this project was a power station which was built on the south bank of the Liffey. A mill race of around 1,600 metres long was constructed, providing water for the turbine which served the dual purpose of generating electricity as well as powering a pump. This pumped water to the specially constructed 37 metre-high water tower, of Italianate design and with a clock, on the western side of the estate. Later a rhyme came into local parlance:

> *Mister Guinness had a clock*
> *And on its top a weather cock*
> *To show the people Castleknock*

The bridge was an integral part of the works: it carried the water pipes and power lines across the river to the house and water tower. Though no known records of construction exist it seems likely that the bridge was built at the same time as the water tower which dates from 1880. No architect or designer is acknowledged for either bridge or tower, though Thomas Henry Wyatt, architect of St Bartholomew's Church on Clyde Road in Dublin, was known to be connected with the house extension and has been mooted for design of the tower. Construction of the bridge was by the engineering department of the Guinness Brewery.

Not content with pure functionality, the arched masonry portal at the northern abutment of the Farmleigh Bridge was designed with decorative

Left: The Italianate Clock Tower at Farmleigh. It overlooks the Liffey and the Farmleigh Bridge. It dates from 1880 and houses a water tank of over 8,000 litres capacity, the water being pumped up from the nearby river. The clock has two faces, each with a diameter of over four metres. This was made by Messrs Grubb of Rathmines, the noted instrument and telescope-makers.

Right: a magnificent stately home – Farmleigh House. The estate was purchased in 1872 by Edward Cecil Guinness, later Lord Iveagh. The original house here was small and was rebuilt and expanded by the Guinnesses.

flair, in the same Italianate style as the tower. Gates were added at either end. However these personified the social and class barriers which underpinned the workings of Victorian society – the bridge was for the exclusive use of the family and their guests and the gates were otherwise locked. Leaving their cottage homes in Palmerstown each day, kitchen staff, farm workers, gardeners and maids went across the Waterstown fields and crossed the Liffey by the ferry which operated there until the 1940s. Tragedy on the river prompted a review of the 'family only' policy for the bridge. An estate worker, Joe Williams, drowned one wild, stormy night as he awaited the ferry home. From then on the bridge was opened to the workers.

Today, surrounded by meadowland, it's easy to see from whence the name Farmleigh came. Even in its first guise as the gentleman's residence of Charles Trench and then John Childley Coote, some acres of the estate were reserved for tillage and others for meadow – the farm and leigh where generations of farm hands put their shoulders to the wheel.

Though its present character has been ravaged somewhat by the passage of time the bridge retains a timeless, ghostly elegance. When shiny and new, the bridge and the river must have seemed as one, smooth and silvery in the summer sun and moodily grey on a winter's day. Today, it is rusted and rustic. When viewed from the road it is the bridge to nowhere on one side and disappears intriguingly through the carved stone portal on the other. Beneath, swans glide silently by and one can almost hear the echo of times past when the Guinness children may have danced across its wooden deck to picnic by the river below. It was, and forever will be, a monument to Victorian industry, inventiveness and timeless romance.

Farmleigh estate was sold to the Irish State in 1999. A major refurbishment followed of the house along with the clock tower, garden, dairy and boathouse. The estate opened to the public in 2001.

Left: with the decorative stone portal partly obscured by trees on the rising ground to the left, the Farmleigh Bridge presents a dramatic vista over the river.

Right: A pedestrian's-eye view of the now skeletal bridge, looking towards the Farmleigh Estate. Rusting and devoid of a walkway surface, the bridge is awaiting a major refurbishment.

Left: Victorian engineers always added decoration to their designs, as demonstrated by the masonry portal at the abutment on the (northern) Farmleigh Estate side of the bridge. The decorative stonework here has some similarities to that on the nearby Italianate Clock Tower (page 30).

The Structure

Farmleigh Bridge is a single-span, wrought-iron attice truss structure on rock-face cut limestone supports. It was constructed around 1880 to carry electricity cables and water pipes from the mill race turbine to the Farmleigh Estate on the north bank of the river. The designer is unknown. Its total length is 52 metres and the original design allowed for gates at either end, with the north gate encased in a decorated stone portal. Presently it is in need of refurbishment. The last work undertaken here was in April 2007 when handrails were erected within the bridge superstructure. However there is no walkway at present and it is inaccessible to the public.

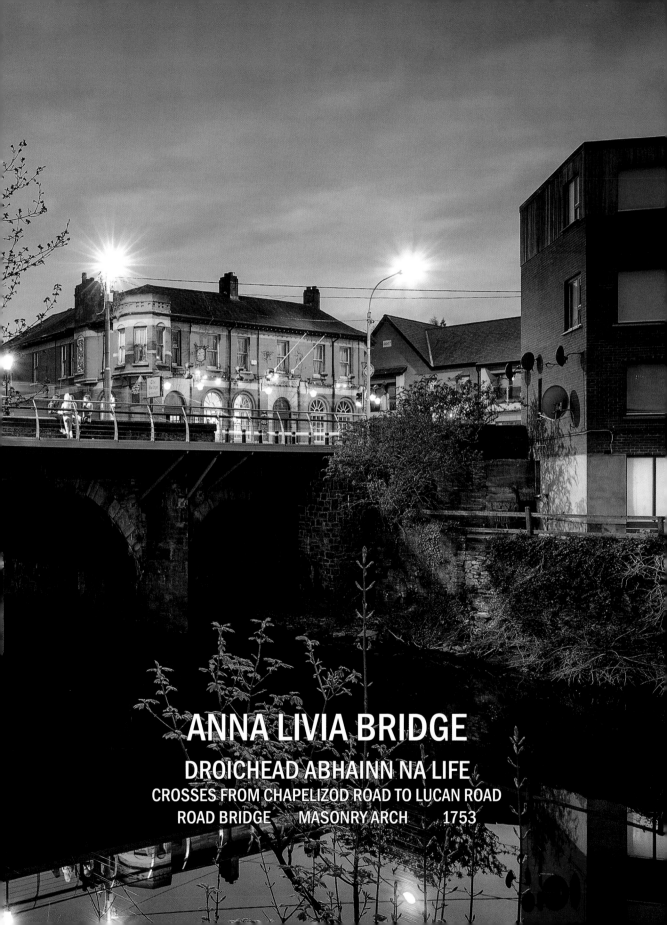

ANNA LIVIA BRIDGE

DROICHEAD ABHAINN NA LIFE
CROSSES FROM CHAPELIZOD ROAD TO LUCAN ROAD
ROAD BRIDGE   MASONRY ARCH   1753

Above: surrounded by the buildings of Chapelizod, old and new, Anna Livia Bridge as seen from the air.

Even the name of this bridge speaks of originality – for Anna Livia is the spirit of the River Liffey, a goddess of rebirth and renewal and her long, flowing hair is the river itself. This tumbles down from the heathery boglands of the Wicklow mountains, curls through a once sleepy Chapelizod and finally parts the city of Dublin into north and south, before joining the Irish Sea.

This most unique bridge at the heart of Chapelizod was renamed Anna Livia Bridge on 16th June 1982. The occasion marked the centenary of the birth of James Joyce who reached deep into the annals of Irish history to source his matriarchal heroine, Anna Livia Plurabelle. She is his 'present from the past' – records of *Abhainn Liphthe* or *Avenlif* exist from as early as the 1st century AD. Perhaps Joyce chose her as he lay musing here on the banks of the Liffey at Chapelizod, a place with which his family had connections. Joyce's father, a businessman of unlucky provenance, had interests in the Chapelizod Distillery. Its downfall preceded the bankruptcy of Joyce's father and the many trials and tribulations of the Joyce family which followed.

Records as far back as the mid-14th century tell of a crossing here – it is unknown whether it was a simple ford or a rough stone structure. The Down Survey of 1656 to 1658, the first detailed land survey of a country ever taken, details a mere ford at Chapelizod. We know also that William Dodson, an English 17th-century engineer, architect and surveyor, was chosen as designer and contractor of a new bridge here at Chapelizod.

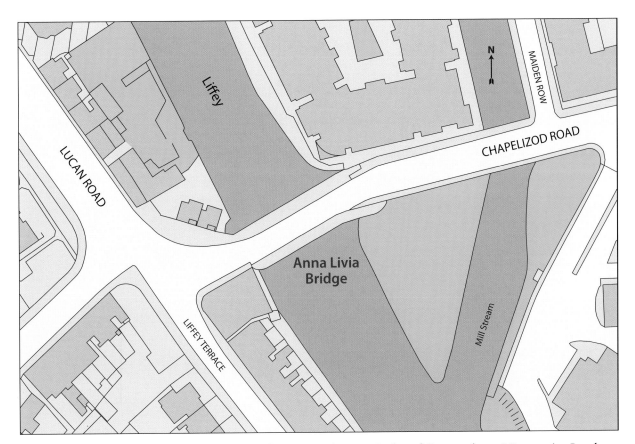

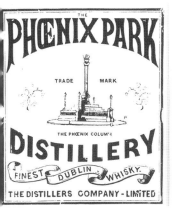

The advent of James Butler, 1st Duke of Ormonde, as Viceroy (or Lord Lieutenant – the British King's representative in Ireland at that time) was to have a lasting effect on Dublin. His tenure in the position (1662-9 and 1677-85) coincided in a great surge in Dublin's expansion and development. As Viceroy, his official residence was in Dublin Castle but it offered only rudimentary accommodation. His out-of-town residence was by the river at Chapelizod. This location, nestling in a scenic valley, offered him luxurious living, deer hunting in the Phoenix Park and clean air, away from the plagues which regularly swept through the city. King William of Orange stayed here en route from his triumph over King James at the Battle of the Boyne in 1690, and Ormonde's manor-house truly merited the name 'King's House'.

Completed at a cost of 195 guineas, 1 shilling and 7 pennies, the 'new' bridge opened in the late 1660s. In style and structure the bridge – for a while known as Dodson's Bridge – was substantially the same as the stone structure we see today, crossing the Liffey in a sweep of four semi-circular arches: made up of two large central arches, flanked on either side by a smaller one giving a total span of 35 metres.

Dodson, though of impressive reputation as an engineer and architect, did not fare as well as his namesake bridge. He had received the substantial sum of 6,000 guineas for walling in the Phoenix Park and had accepted a post as 'farmer of beer and ale' in Ireland – an ancient term for excise commissioner. When his none-too-well constructed park wall began to collapse, so too his

Above: with sailors in attendance, a helmetted diver drags the river by the bridge for the weapon used in the 1882 Phoenix Park assasinations – as depicted by the 'Illustrated London News'. The assassins had fled by way of the bridge.

Left: etching of the older bridge built in the 1660s – known for a while as 'Dodson's Bridge'.

world came tumbling down. His crime had not been so much to milk the public purse while producing substandard work – this was expected – but the breaches in the wall had allowed the deer to escape and that was inexcusable. Dodson's accounts were examined. Perhaps it was his great affinity for water, and experience of construction by it – he was responsible for large drainage projects in the Netherlands, Germany and the English Fens – but on examining the bridge the commission of enquiry found that it was sufficiently 'done'.

In time the term Dodson's Bridge fell from common usage and 'Chapelizod' became the name of choice. It is a legendary name promising intrigue and romance – the place of the Chapel of Izod, or La Belle Izod, daughter of King Anguish of Ireland and his queen, Iseult the Elder. In this tale, part of mediaeval mythology, Izod is dispatched to marry King Mark of Cornwall. She is accompanied by Tristan, who had slain her mother's brother. The pair drink a love potion and though Izod marries Mark, she answers the dying wish of a mortally wounded Tristan and rushes to his bedside. The legend has it that she died there, her lips on his, and her grieving father brought her body back to Ireland erecting a chapel here in her memory.

The fate of Chapelizod Bridge twists and turns through history and is not always faithfully recorded. It does, however, seem intimately linked with that of the great house, the King's House. A fire at Dublin Castle in 1684 brought about a substantial rebuild of the castle offering more fitting living quarters for the Viceroy. And once the last Viceroy had left the Chapelizod residence the officers of the Royal Irish Regiment of Artillery took up quarters in the house. By the mid-1700s the house of Chapelizod and the bridge had fallen into disrepair. Some rebuilding of the bridge took place in 1753 but by 1792 a visitor wrote that the parapet wall was 'still extremely unsafe', 'extremely diminished by the loss of capping stones being mischievously thrown into the river' and barely sufficient in height to prevent bridge users from falling into the water. Indeed, that same year, one such event was recorded – a young man sitting upon the parapet to rest tumbled into the Liffey below.

It was around this time too that the Royal Irish Regiment of Artillery relocated from Chapelizod to Islandbridge and the village once more became

Left: in 2011 pedestrian walkways, overhanging the river, were fixed to the bridge spandrels.

a quiet backwater, being no longer of interest to those who held the reins of power and the strings of the public purse. We do not know what repairs or new construction that may have taken place here. Nothing of great import happened in Chapelizod and no one remarked upon the village and its bridge. A passing observation, recorded in 1851, draws the forlorn picture of the 'skew arch of the old bridge' still standing. A travelogue of 1856 reflects on Chapelizod as 'once prosperous, with a good broad street, well paved footpath and lofty houses, a humble Catholic church, a steep bridge spanning the Liffey and a great mill' but now in a sad and forlorn condition. It had a 'melancholy picturesqueness' and the bridge had been 'superseded' since the closing of the barracks.

The next glimpse of the bridge comes in 1882 when an engraving in the *Illustrated London News* depicts it in good condition and holding a great crowd of people observing a diver searching the river for the weapon used in the Phoenix Park murders of that year. The principal British officials in Ireland, Lord Frederick Cavendish, the Chief Secretary for Ireland and Thomas Henry Burke, the Permanent Under Secretary, were assassinated by the Invincibles, radical Irish nationalists, while walking in the Phoenix Park. The assassins were observed fleeing by way of Chapelizod Bridge and the forces of law and order quickly descended upon the village. The river bed was searched inch by inch. When no weapons were found, the villagers dispersed down the steep slopes of the bridge and the village once more fell back to its state of quiet sleepiness.

Modern record keeping allows us to follow the recent history of the bridge more closely. Dublin Corporation undertook a major re-grouting project in the 1980s and further strengthened and refurbished it in 1991. That same year a report confirmed that the bridge is a patchwork of 18th- and 19th-century repairs and rebuilds and noted in particular that the north-side arches were of earlier construction, different and inferior to those closest to the south side.

Faced with the dilemma of keeping pedestrian traffic safe on the increasingly-busier bridge while maintaining the historical structure, Dublin City Council commissioned an appropriate new look for Anna Livia (Chapelizod) Bridge. Today walkways fixed to the bridge spandrels overhang the river, marrying the old stone with the simplicity of modern materials and design.

Below: the Mill Race at the Anna Livia Bridge.

Right: the Phoenix Monument, erected by the Earl of Chesterfield in 1747. Carved in Portland stone, it is a phoenix rising from the ashes. It is at the focal point of the main artery of the Park, Chesterfield Avenue. The Chaplelizod (now Anna Livia) Bridge was a strategic point on one of the main roads leading to the Phoenix Park.

The Structure

The Anna Livia Bridge is made up of four semi-circular masonry arches spanning 35 metres with the outer two arches being smaller than the central two. The structure, originally completed in 1753, was refurbished and strengthened by Dublin Corporation in 1991. The voussoirs of the arches are of well-dressed and pointed stones, which appear to be a later addition. The soffit of the arches have been rendered in a smooth cementatious mortar. In modern times, the footpaths on the bridge were found to be too narrow and a safety hazard for pedestrians, considering the volumes of traffic traversing the bridge. In 2011 Dublin City Council constructed two light structural walkways on either side of the bridge.

41

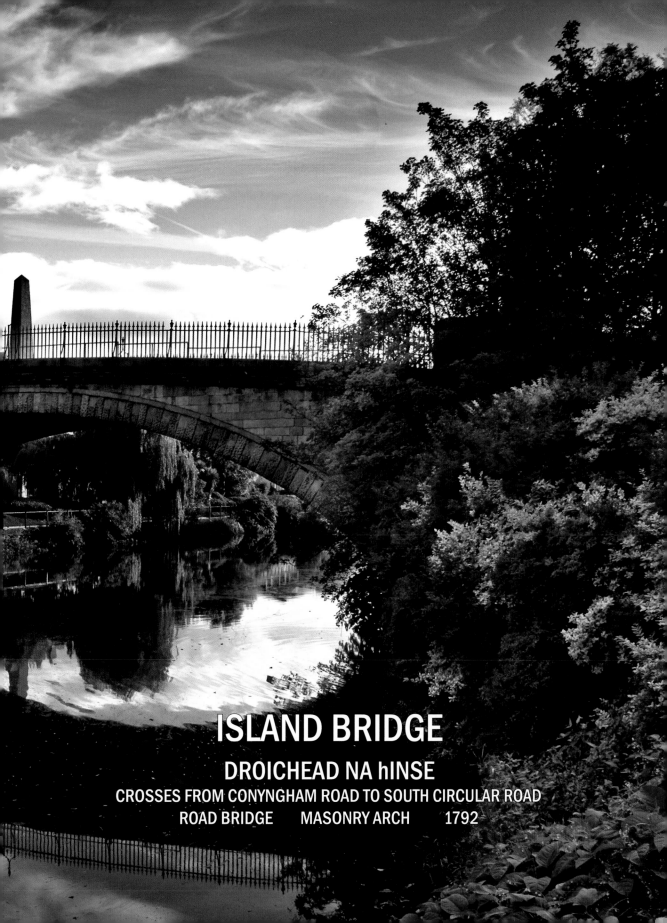

ISLAND BRIDGE

DROICHEAD NA hINSE
CROSSES FROM CONYNGHAM ROAD TO SOUTH CIRCULAR ROAD
ROAD BRIDGE   MASONRY ARCH   1792

R omantic in character and delightfully sylvan in setting, Island Bridge is a discreet yet fascinating gem in the necklace of Liffey bridges. It connects the South Circular Road to Conyngham Road on the north side. Classical in style, with a single, eye pleasing, elliptical arch built of Portland stone, the bridge is complemented by its natural setting: the Phoenix Park on the north side of the river and the lace of overhanging willow and abundant greenery on the river bank itself. Here, having taken its final leave of its origins in the Wicklow mountains, and after its long journey across the Kildare plains, the river turns towards the city to flow under this centuries-old bridge, first known as Sarah Bridge.

Young, beautiful and spirited, Sarah Fane laid the foundation stone of the present Island Bridge on 22nd June 1791. It was to replace an older, crumbling structure known as Sidney's Bridge. As wife of the Viceroy, and thus Ireland's most eminent lady, she was happily undertaking yet another public duty.

Above: an 18th-century view. Sarah Bridge, in the centre, is elegantly framed by the Phoenix Park to the left and the Royal Hospital, Kilmainham to the right.

Right: portrait, dating from 1786, of Sarah Fane, Countess of Westmorland, by Ozias Humphry, a leading 18th-century English painter.

She was no ordinary first lady – her's is the story of swashbuckling romantic novels. As the 17 year-old daughter of one of England's richest men, Sarah was wooed and won by the financially-embarrassed and somewhat socially uncouth John Fane. In January 1782, she slipped from under the disapproving eye of her father, Robert Childs, and the Rubens-painted ceiling of her palatial home and fled with the waiting John. The enraged father was soon in hot pursuit, racing from London with his armed entourage, finally gaining sight of the couple as they neared the Scottish border. In the confusion of a gunfight waged between the rival groomsmen, Sarah and John slipped over the border to Gretna Green watched by her father, now powerless, who promptly disinherited her.

In 1774 John Fane succeeded to the Earldom of Westmorland on the death of his father. He turned out to be politically adept and was appointed Lord Lieutenant in Ireland in 1789. He brought Sarah and their young family to reside in the Phoenix Park where as Vicereine she led a life of privilege and influence. Wherever Sarah charmingly bestowed her attentions, Dublin

Above: Island Bridge seen from the air.

society gaily followed. She had, of course, the duty of declaring her namesake bridge open in October 1792. But Sarah died, very young – most likely a victim of a cholera epidemic, in November 1793. Her last journey from the Phoenix Park to burial in the family mausoleum in England passed over the bridge named in her honour.

Alexander Stevens, the designer of the bridge, had ensured no expense had been spared on what was then, at 32 metres span, the longest single arch masonry bridge in Ireland. The bridge was adorned with elegant lamp standards: one on each of its four piers and others along its length. Much praised for the elegance of its design and standard of workmanship, it was favourably compared with the Rialto Bridge in Venice. Artists, amateur and professional, pronounced it a fine location for sketching the river against a backdrop of the Phoenix Park and Islandbridge and its surrounds. For some time after its opening, the ghostly structure of Sidney's Bridge remained in the background – it was finally demolished in 1793.

The Phoenix Park, always a popular place for the city's population to retreat to, became even busier once the bridge provided safe access from the South Circular Road. Although it was Elizabeth I who originally conceived the idea of a large deer park for Dublin, it was the Viceroy, James Butler, Duke of Ormonde who undertook its development. At first, the park was exclusively for the cream of society, however it opened to the general public in the mid-1700s. The Phoenix spa in the glen, near the entrance to the Vice-regal residence, once the home of Sarah Fane, was a popular place to sip the waters whether one paid the premium price of five shillings for a seat in the rustic dome, or a penny for a cup to take away. Military reviews, frequently

Below: another view of the bridge with the Royal Hospital to the right.

Right: map of the Island Bridge and surrounding area.

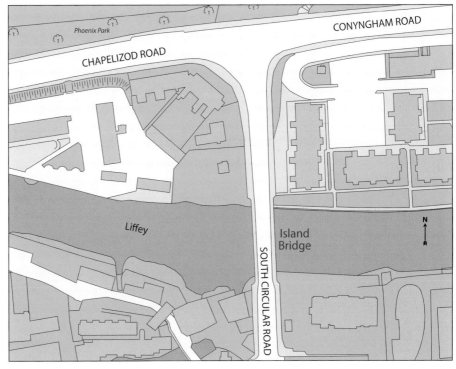

Below: elegant and practical – detail of the springing at Island Bridge.

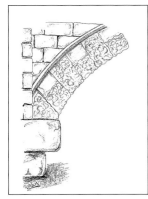

conducted in the park, offered particular entertainment or one could blithely stroll through the encampments to see and be seen. At other times, soldiers enacted mock battles, which spilt down to the banks of the Liffey and onto the bridge itself.

The area of Islandbridge was strategically important – the walled city, the stronghold of power, lay to the east and wild, open lawless country to the west, where in 1013, Brian Boru camped during his siege of Dublin. Strongbow, the Norman conqueror, dallied here to found the priory of Kilmainham in 1174 and Silken Thomas galloped through on his whistle-stop tour to garner support for his doomed rebellion against the English in 1534. History's most infamous husband, Henry VIII, cast his shadow upon this land, deeming the priory his own when he ruthlessly dissolved the monasteries.

In old and medieval Dublin when the good friars of Kilmainham still inhabited the priory this was a place of mill races and salmon fisheries where Kilmahonock's Ford, most likely of mud or wattle, straddled the river. As the English grip tightened on the city and country the need for a more secure crossing became urgent. The first stone bridge, built in the mid-15th century, was washed away by floods in 1545.

A replacement bridge, Sidney's Bridge, a commanding structure of eight arches and regally embellished with the insignia of Queen Elizabeth I, opened in 1577. Sir Henry Sidney was Queen Elizabeth's man in Ireland charged with a mission to ruthlessly suppress dissent and to impose English law and custom on the native lords. He succeeded in bringing some of the Irish clans under his control, against the others he raged a vicious war. The bridge was crucial to controlling access to the city, a function it served for over 200 years

during which time Islandbridge also became a place of industry. Flour mills, breweries, fisheries and bleachers flourished along the river. The clean waters of the Liffey, upstream of the filthy, disease-ridden city, were prized for their health-giving properties and were channelled across the bridge through wooden pipes by means of a 'forcing engine' in the 1730s.

Despite its importance, by the late 18th century Sidney's Bridge was in a dilapidated state. Parliament in London was intensively lobbied for funds for a new structure. A first attempt in the early 1780s failed – corruption and mismanagement resulted in all monies granted being spent with nothing to show but half-built abutments and two lone pillars in mid-river. The floods of 1787, cascading from the mountains to the sea, took with them three arches of Sidney's Bridge and a young boy, driving home in darkness, plunged into the river.

Improvised repairs were made using timber trusses and a temporary wooden deck – the fractured water pipe being of urgent concern. Finally, parliament once more advanced monies for the new bridge; Sarah Bridge, which has served the city well to this day. The structure has undergone few repairs: the flag footpaths retain the original arch profile, though the road has been lowered with a less pronounced arch facilitating modern traffic.

In 1922 as the newly independent Irish State shook off its centuries-long colonial shackles, it decried too the romance and intrigue in Sarah's story and gave us the new name: Island Bridge.

Above: in previous centuries, the elegance of the design of Island Bridge, as well as its perfect riverine location led to it being the centre-piece of many paintings and engravings. This early 19th-century sketch by Samuel Frederick Brocas clearly shows the bridge in its full detail, without the mantle of latter-day buildings which now generally obscure it. It is a perfect foil to the imposing Wellington Monument, seen to the left.

The Structure

The foundation stone for Island Bridge, or Sarah Bridge as it was known then, was laid in June 1791. Designed and constructed by Alexander Stevens, a Scottish engineer, the work was also supervised by Edward Cope and the project was managed by John Blaquiere. Cope reported on progress and completion that "Stevens spared no expense to complete the whole of the work properly". He also makes mention of a "dam-head" which would suggest that the abutment foundations were constructed inside some type of cofferdam, probably similar to Semple's Essex Bridge of 1755.

Spanning the Liffey between Conyngham Road to the north and the South Circular Road, it is an attractive single-span elliptical arched bridge (the second longest in Ireland, after Lucan Bridge) composed of evenly coursed granite ashlar. The parapet comprises four large granite dadoes and fourteen sections of ornamental wrought-iron railings. The crown is nine metres above low water. The flag footpaths retain the original arch profile though the road has been lowered somewhat to give a less pronounced arch.

It is described by Ted Ruddock, in his seminal book *Arch Bridges and their Builders 1735-1835*, as "a single arch of bastard elliptical shape and 31 metre span, which was built in 1791-1792. It bears no resemblance to Stevens' earlier bridges except those of competent design and construction. It is of generous width, almost 12 metres and fenced with an iron handrail which was probably erected when first built".

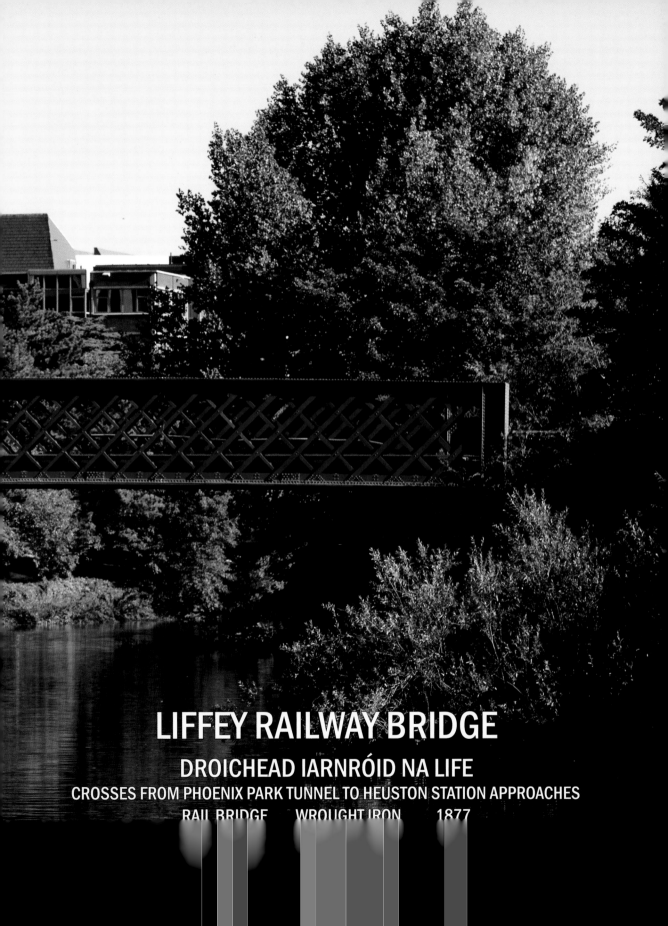

LIFFEY RAILWAY BRIDGE

DROICHEAD IARNRÓID NA LIFE

CROSSES FROM PHOENIX PARK TUNNEL TO HEUSTON STATION APPROACHES

RAIL BRIDGE   WROUGHT IRON   1877

The Liffey Railway Bridge spans the river from a point west of the Heuston Railway Station complex on the south side of the river towards the Phoenix Park railway tunnel on the north side. The bridge accomodates two tracks. Trains can approach from Heuston's number 10 platform and travel onto the bridge, under the adjacent road bridge at Conyngham Road and directly enter the tunnel.

The bridge was constructed for the Great Southern and Western Railway (GS&WR). Designed in 1874, it was complete for the opening of the GS&WR branch to North Wall in 1877. The construction of the central span is riveted and of wrought iron, a typical bridge-building material of the time. The span over the river is of lattice-girder design, a type which was developed in Ireland. County Louth-born Sir John MacNeill, is credited by the British Institution of Civil Engineers as 'the engineer who introduced iron lattice bridges into the United Kingdom.' His first pioneering example was the 47 metre-span lattice-girder bridge over the Royal Canal at Dublin for the Dublin & Drogheda Railway. At an early stage in his career, he was the assistant of Thomas Telford, the noted British Civil Engineer. In 1842 he became the first Professor 'of the Practice of Engineering' at Trinity College Dublin.

The wrought-iron Liffey Railway Bridge has a span of 34 metres over the river and rests on cast iron bearings sitting on masonry abutments. Partially hidden from view by vegetation are three semi-circular masonry arches on either side, of five metre spans each – giving a total combined length of bridge of 64 metres. Intriguingly the builders left behind some traces of their 19th-

Above: the railway line traverses the river over the Liffey Railway Bridge, and then disappears from sight under Conyngham Road into the portal of the Phoenix Park Tunnel.

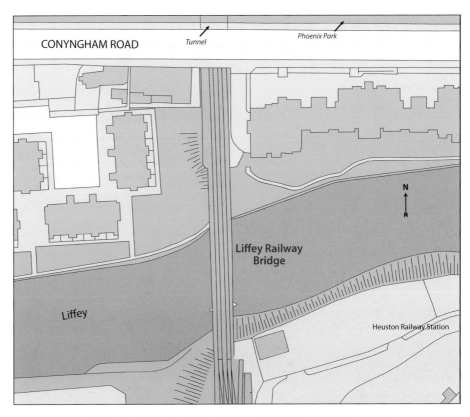

century methodologies – timber sheet piles around the southern abutment suggest the employment of cofferdams – temporary watertight structures allowing underwater foundations to be built in dry conditions.

Much bridge construction was being considered in the Dublin of the 1860s and 1870s. Plans were afoot for the remodelling of Essex Bridge (now Grattan Bridge), the widening of the Carlisle Bridge (now O'Connell Bridge) and some were even demanding a new bridge in the vicinity of the Custom House. Part of the consideration was the cost of these road bridges – not popular with reluctant Victorian taxpayers. In the case of the railways, still experiencing the later stages of a 'railway mania', promoters invested money in new lines, in the expectation of profit. Thus, in the case of bridges such as the Liffey Railway Bridge, it was financed not from the coffers of the state or city but from those of railway companies. Two opposing proposals had emerged in the 1860s for railway bridges spanning the Liffey from the vicinity of Kingsbridge (Heuston) Station – one envisaged an eight-arch structure with each arch a little over nine metres long and another a viaduct of around 52 metres in length.

The requirement for this bridge came from the need for the GS&WR to reach the Dublin quays, as well as to connect with the Midland Great Western Railway (MGWR), whose terminus was at Broadstone. Impetus was given by the plans of the London & North Western Railway to operate a packet steamer service from Dublin to Holyhead. The new connection was built, from the approaches to Kingsbridge, then crossed the Liffey, went under

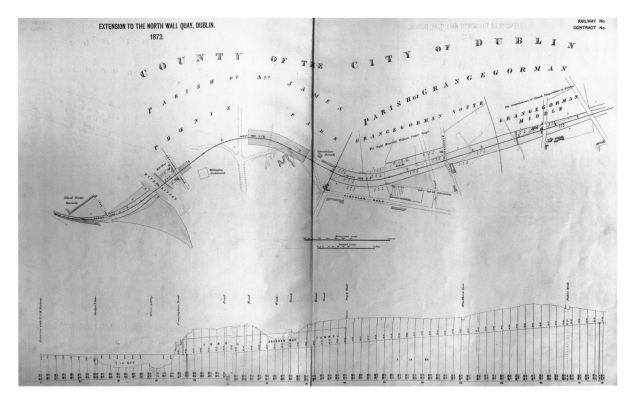

the Phoenix Park through a tunnel, to Glasnevin, where the line first passed under, and linked to the North Wall quay, via the MGWR connections which had been in place since 1864. When complete, rail traffic could be connected to the steamer services to Britain and beyond from the south and the west via the GS&WR network.

The route, as well as construction of the Liffey Railway Bridge, also necessitated the building of a 692 metre-long tunnel under the Phoenix Park. The tunnel has its place in Irish history. In 1916, on the outbreak of the Rising at midday on Easter Monday, 24th April, British troops were rapidly dispatched by train from the Curragh camp in Co. Kildare. By around 5 pm some 1,600 had disembarked at Kingsbridge, save one train which went via the Phoenix Park tunnel to North Wall to reinforce the guard over the docks. During World War II – a time known as the 'Emergency' in Ireland – food supplies were taken by train into the tunnel where they were stored.

Today, the link is used mainly for rail freight, though the route is used for passenger trains on occasions when unusually large volumes of passengers are experienced, such as the days of All Ireland Finals. With consideration of its future use for passenger traffic, work is underway to upgrade this branch line through the tunnel.

The Liffey Railway Bridge is designated Underbridge 1, North Wall – Great Southern Branch, under the Iarnród Éireann bridge numbering system. It is one of 3,094 railway bridges in Ireland, with 1,906 being under-bridges, i.e. a bridge under the railway track and 1,188 being over-bridges, i.e., a bridge over the railway. Around 30% are of steel or iron construction (like the Liffey Railway Bridge), the rest are of masonry or concrete construction.

Above: plan for the railway extension to North Wall. The bridge over the Liffey is shown on the left. Next is the tunnel under the Phoenix Park. The cross-section at the bottom illustrates the heights through the tunnel. In the event, some of the route had to be tunneled under the park, the rest was by cut and cover construction.

Below: GS&WR insignia.

54

Above: a General Motors diesel locomotive crosses the bridge. The lattice girder of the bridge is slightly cambered as can be seen in this photograph.

Right: framed by the masonry arch of Island Bridge – the railway bridge downriver.

Left: a triumph of connectivity – the Liffey Railway Bridge carries twin tracks over the river from the Phoenix Park Tunnel (and the line from Connolly Station and the docks) to the approaches to Heuston Station, and onwards to the railway network in the south and west.

The Structure

The Liffey Railway Bridge is a seven-span structure, the central span of 34 metres being of lattice girders of wrought-iron riveted construction. At either end of this central span the girders rest on cast-iron bearings on masonry abutments. On either side, on the approach to the central span there are three masonry arches of five metres span each. The foundations appear to be on rock without piles and the evidence of timber sheet piles visible around the south side abutment suggest they were built using cofferdams. This railway underbridge was constructed for the Great Southern and Western Railway and completed in 1877.

Chapter 2
THE MIDDLE LIFFEY
RÉIMSE LÁRNACH NA LIFE

Sculpted keystone on O'Donovan Rossa Bridge

We follow the course of the Liffey as it runs through the heart of Dublin. First we encounter King's (now Seán Heuston) Bridge in all its cast-iron finery, now adapted to carry the Luas. Then, after an iconoclastic bridge by Calatrava, we come to a series of centuries-old bridges, central to the history of the city. Finally we reach the most emblematic of them all: the Ha'penny Bridge, exemplar of the Industrial Revolution. In its simplicity and elegance, it has become a symbol of Dublin.

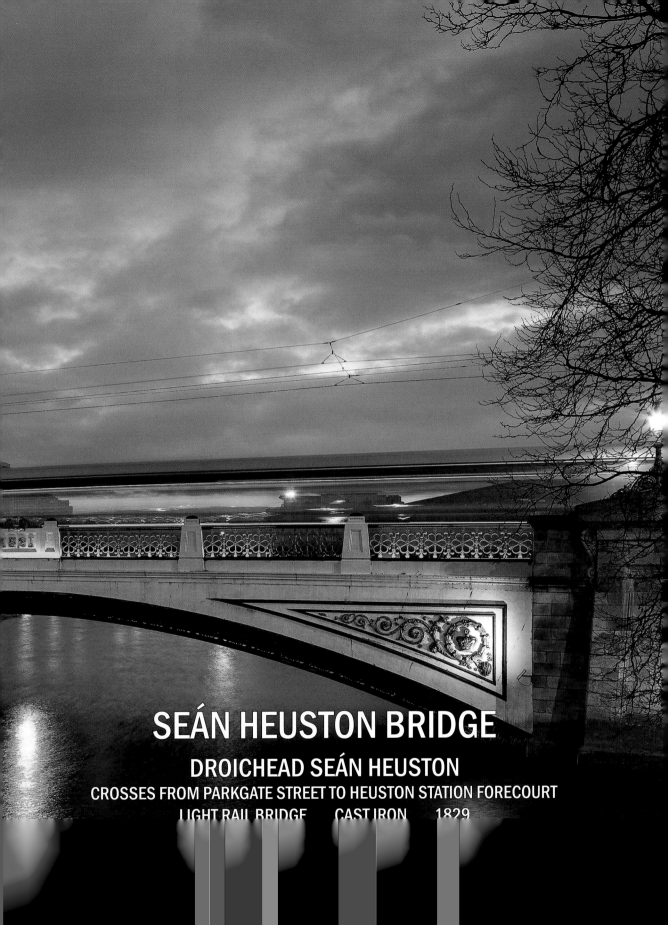

SEÁN HEUSTON BRIDGE

DROICHEAD SEÁN HEUSTON

CROSSES FROM PARKGATE STREET TO HEUSTON STATION FORECOURT

LIGHT RAIL BRIDGE   CAST IRON   1829

Left: *aerial view of the Seán Heuston Bridge, as it was in 1982 – then a road bridge. The refurbished bridge is now exclusively for the Luas and pedestrians.*

Seán Heuston Bridge is the very model of an old city bridge being put to excellent use in modern times. It links the north and south quays near the commanding, Italianate Heuston Railway Station and carries the *Luas* light rail system on its journey from the western suburbs of Tallaght and Saggart to the Point area on the city's eastern flank. The bridge is also open to pedestrians.

When building commenced in 1827 the location was a quiet one on the western fringes of the bustling city. The Liffey here was not yet embanked or enclosed by quays. Grassy meadows ran down to the muddy waterfront at this spot. Overlooking the river on the south bank was Dr Steeven's Hospital and to the north the Phoenix Park offered city dwellers a verdant retreat from the congested streets. Looming large in one corner of this otherwise idyllic scene was Richard Robinson's Phoenix Iron Works. It was here where the new bridge was fabricated in 1827 at a cost of £13,000. The design was by George Papworth (1781-1855).

The bridge was paid for by public subscription by Dubliners to commemorate George IV's visit to Dublin in 1821, which had been deemed a resounding success. Dubliners have always been enthusiastic about royal visits and the portly king had won the hearts of his subjects. It was decided that the city should have a fitting memorial to that visit. Daniel O'Connell was at the helm of the fundraising though he initially thought a royal palace was a more fitting tribute – but Dubliners' pockets were not quite that deep and in any case there were only 200,000 of them then! The king himself chose the design from a selection submitted to him.

Such was the prestige of the project that Marquis Wellesley (brother of the Duke of Wellington), suitably attired in a gold trimmed, white satin apron, laid the foundation stone in December 1827 – a duty he performed with the aid of a ruby- and emerald-studded trowel, engraved with a depiction of the soon-to-be-built bridge which he declared to be the 'bridge of George

Below: seen under a light layer of snow, the date of King George IV's visit is still proclaimed, with an emblem of feathers atop, the heraldic badge of the Prince of Wales.

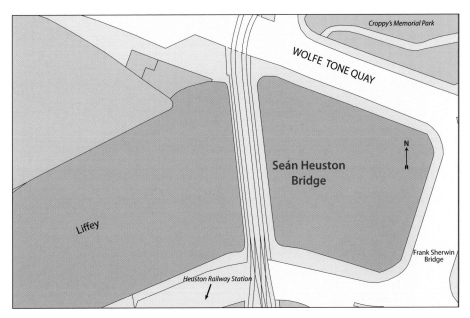

The map shows labels: Croppy's Memorial Park, WOLFE TONE QUAY, Seán Heuston Bridge, Liffey, Frank Sherwin Bridge, Heuston Railway Station, N.

the Fourth' – which translated in Dublin parlance to the 'Kingsbridge'. The bridge opened on 9th June 1829, as recorded on the central upright of the balustrade.

Many of the bridge's features boast of its royal associations. The single arch is decoratively edged with a repeated design of feathers, the heraldic badge of the Prince of Wales. The spandrels on either side are regally embellished with wreath-enclosed crowns and majestic, golden swirls. The original plan included a triumphal central arch but this was not proceeded with – possibly for cost reasons. The date tablet was originally topped with yet more crowns.

It was a toll bridge and the toll accrued to Richard Robinson of the ironworks, who magnanimously donated the first day's takings to the Mendicity Institution, a charity for Dublin's homeless. Ironically, Seán Heuston led the garrison which occupied this institution during the 1916 Rising, heroically defending it for three days.

The only loser in this tale of a king and his bridge was Dr Steeven's Hospital which had benefitted from the profits of a ferry which had plied its trade upon this stretch of Liffey water for over 100 years before the bridge opened.

Possibly Ireland's oldest cast-iron road bridge, Seán Heuston Bridge has seven iron arch ribs and a span of 30 metres. It is a little over nine metres wide and is supported by tapering granite abutments on each side. Given the short construction period it is most likely that piles were not used in the abutments but that the foundations for the abutment were placed directly on the underlying rock. The Liffey, in those times, approached the city in a sinuous curve beyond the bridge. Later in 1843, a new channel was cut for the river between the Kingsbridge and Barrack (now Rory O'More) Bridge. Upper and lower dams were built at either bridge and the river walls and quays were constructed. On 6th May 1844, the upper and lower dams were cut through and within 15 minutes the Liffey flowed freely again.

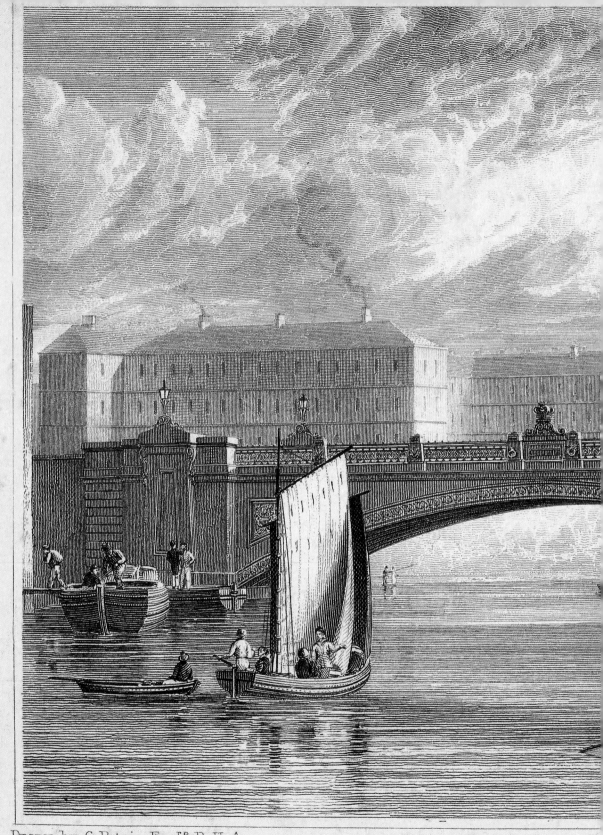

Drawn by G. Petrie, Esqre R.H.A.

THE KING'S BRIDGE, DUBLIN,

TO HIS MOST GRACIOUS MAJESTY, GEOR

Engraved by T. Higham.

ST VIEW) & ROYAL BARRACKS.

Seán Heuston Bridge has withstood the test of time – although, after a structural analysis, Dublin Corporation placed a load restriction of two tonnes on the bridge in 1980. In tandem with this the Corporation also commissioned a new relief bridge for the area, the Frank Sherwin Bridge, construction of which began in the same year.

In 2001 a €4 million refurbishment project got underway and was completed in 2002. As part of this initiative, led by the Railway Procurement Agency, the cast iron and granite were thoroughly cleaned of almost two centuries of city grime, the cast-iron girders were replaced and a new deck was constructed to carry the *Luas*.

The bridge is now named for Captain Seán Heuston and is the only Liffey bridge to be named for an executed hero of the 1916 Rising. Heuston was a Dubliner and his remarkable mother Maria, and his aunts Teresa and Brigid had somehow seen to it that he received an exceptional standard of education for a tenement child. For his part in the Easter Rising Seán Heuston (aged 25) was tried by Field General Courts Martial on Thursday 4th May 1916. His death sentence was confirmed by General Sir John Maxwell. At Kilmainham Gaol, at dawn on Monday 8th May a small square of white paper was pinned to his coat over his heart and he was executed by firing squad. The bridge was renamed in his honour in 1941. It is a fitting location as Heuston had worked for the GS&WR at the nearby Kingsbridge railway station (also renamed for him in 1966).

Previous to that the bridge had been called the Patrick Sarsfield Bridge – renamed in 1922, British rule in Ireland having been toppled in 1921, along with the crowns atop the King's Bridge. Sarsfield was the very essence of a 17th-century hero – tall, well-travelled, a duellist full of derring-do, a ladies' man and always true to his ideals. Exiled from Ireland following the Williamite Wars of 1689 to 1691, he died in 1693 on the battlefields of Belgium in the cause of Louis XIV. However the name – Sarsfield Bridge – was little used by Dubliners.

One of the more decorous bridges over the Liffey, with its elegant cast-iron sides, the Seán Heuston Bridge is a favourite of many a Dubliner who, showing their long memories, even today still refer to the 'Kingsbridge'.

Above: beneath opulent and decorative gilt, the plaque proclaims that it is 'Droichead Seán Heuston'. Heuston was one of the leaders of the Easter Rising, which hastened the break-up of an empire.

Right: Heuston Railway Station is framed by the bridge and by the overhead catenary of the Luas system.

Below: the bridge is now named after Captain Seán Heuston, who led the Volunteer detachment that fought at the Mendicity Institution, located just down the quays, during Easter 1916.

KING'S BRIDGE & TERMINUS. DUBLIN. 9. W.L.

Above: in a major refurbishment commencing in 2001, the original cast iron arch ribs were replaced by curved steel girders. The cast-iron fascia panels and parapets were retained.

Left: the decorative cast-iron fascia panels next to the granite abutment of Seán Heuston Bridge.

Right: the refurbished and strengthened bridge now carries two Luas tracks and a footpath.

Left: the bridge as it was at the end of the 19th century. The receding granite abutments are built to an Egyptian theme (similar in style to the façade of Broadstone Station), popular in the late Georgian and early Victorian eras. Note the crown over the '1821' plaque. Compare it with the present-day photograph (page 60): post-independence, the crown was removed.

The Structure

Seán Heuston Bridge is an ornate, single-span arch structure of cast iron with granite abutments which were most likely laid directly on the underlying rock without the use of piles. Originally it had seven cast-iron arched ribs of 30 metres span with the outer fascias being highly decorated. The parapets and dadoes are also of cast iron. It was designed by the Dublin-based architect George Papworth. The Phoenix Iron Works, nearby at Parkgate Street, supplied the castings and undertook the erection of the bridge which took less than one year to complete. It opened in June 1829.

In the 1980s a load restriction of two tonnes was placed upon the bridge – and the adjacent Frank Sherwin Bridge was built to carry the traffic. A €4 million refurbishment of the bridge began in 2001 as part of the *Luas* light rail project. The cast iron and granite was cleaned, the cast-iron arch ribs were replaced with steel girders and a new deck was laid. The first tram crossed Seán Heuston Bridge in 2004.

FRANK SHERWIN BRIDGE

DROICHEAD PHROINSIAS UÍ SHEARBHÁIN

CROSSES FROM WOLFE TONE QUAY TO VICTORIA QUAY

ROAD BRIDGE   CONCRETE   1982

The Frank Sherwin Bridge straddles the River Liffey a mere 65 metres to the east of the unique and historic Seán Heuston Bridge. By contrast to the older bridge, it is in a modern and utilitarian style. It was designed with a low profile and open appearance so as not to crowd the river view, to complement the streetscape and to fulfil the necessary and, at the time, urgent function of improving the traffic flow on Dublin's quays. Utilising a one-way system, its four lanes carry traffic from Victoria Quay and the Heuston Station area to Wolfe Tone Quay on the north river bank. There also are footpaths for pedestrians.

Above: aerial view of the Frank Sherwin Bridge as it was just after its opening (middle of photograph). It was built as a relief bridge for the nearby Seán Heuston Bridge (top of photograph) after a load restriction was placed on this in 1980 and formed part of a major traffic improvement initiative.

The initial proposal for the bridge was made in 1977. Traffic along the quays had increased exponentially which, in the era before the M50 provided an outer relief route, were among the main arterial routes in and out of the city. Heavy goods vehicles in particular made their way to and from the port along the quays. Traffic jams were commonplace. There were concerns too for the structural integrity of the 160 year-old Seán Heuston Bridge which was suffering due to the heavy traffic. In 1980 the decision was taken by Dublin Corporation to close it to vehicles in excess of two tonnes. In the same year construction of the Frank Sherwin bridge commenced.

Dubliners were not so used to witnessing bridge construction on the river. The first new bridge built for 46 years had commenced down river by Gandon's majestic Custom House a mere four years previously. This, the Talbot Memorial Bridge, which opened in 1978 was in profile and function a sister bridge of the Frank Sherwin Bridge.

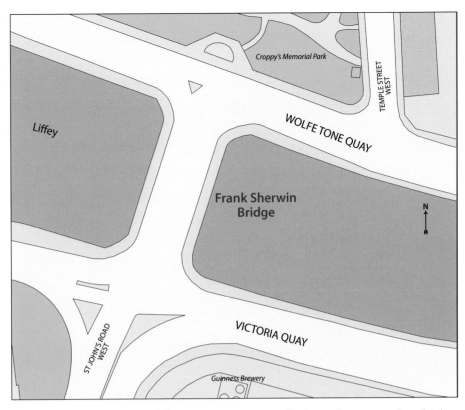

Given the urgent need for a new crossing to facilitate heavy goods vehicles and the straitened economic times, the design brief emphasised simplicity of construction and cost – though aesthetics were also a factor. Designed 'in house' by Richard Fowler of the Roads Design Section of Dublin Corporation, the build time was as remarkably quick as the design to commencement stage.

Interlocking sheet-piled cofferdams provided dry areas upon the riverbed in which to construct the piers. Standing on rock foundations, these geometrically shaped piers were arranged in two groups of three and support the three spans of the bridge. The centre span is the longest at 22 metres and each side span is of 14 metres. The four traffic lanes and two pedestrian footpaths give a bridge width of just under 20 metres. The deck was cast in situ and is of reinforced concrete.

A workaday bridge, the profile and proportions of the bridge are understated – this allows the eye to wander to the city beyond – and the granite dusting on the upper panels of the bridge soften its overall appearance. The traditional three-arch effect was achieved by varying the thickness of the deck, whilst setting the piers back from the bridge face contributed to its overall slender look.

The opening of the bridge was quite a major event for Dublin – as not only would traffic traverse the bridge for the first time but traffic flow on the quays was to be reversed. Cognisant of the harried motorist, Dublin Corporation timed the change for Sunday, 29th August 1982. The meticulously planned operation – which cost £200,000 – began in the early morning

under the curious gaze of the few Dubliners who were out and about. Within a 15 minute period a team of Dublin Corporation workers closed the quays to all vehicles, unveiled 300 new traffic signs and inaugurated nine new traffic islands. Traffic lights immediately synchronised with the new flows as the switchover had involved the computerisation of all traffic lights within the city area. A total of ten kilometres of city streets were affected by the new arrangements with traffic on the north quays now flowing eastwards towards the docklands and travel was now in a westerly direction on the south quays. The appliance of the relatively new science of urban traffic management dictated that 'conflict points' where opposing traffic flows cross each other, should be reduced to a minimum – and the Frank Sherwin Bridge was pivotal to that.

Though there was a certain amount of head scratching and finger waving by uninitiated commuters the benefits were soon felt as typical half hour crawls along the quays were radically reduced.

The bridge was named for Frank Sherwin, a Dubliner, a councillor in Dublin Corporation and an independent representative in Dáil Éireann for

Above: cameras roll at the opening ceremony in 1982. The opening of the bridge allowed traffic management in central Dublin to be radically re-organised. Traffic on the north quays could now flow eastwards, while that on the south quays travelled westwards.

Right: note the tapered design of this row of concrete piers, one of two rows in the river.

eight years from 1957. Born in 1905 in his family's one room tenement on Dorset Street, Sherwin bore witness to every major event of the 20th century from the Lockout of 1913, the Easter Rising of 1916 to events later in the century such as Ireland joining the European Union in 1973. Frank Sherwin fought in the War of Independence of 1919 to 1921. By 17 years of age he was a veteran urban guerrilla. Fighting for the anti-Treaty side in the Civil War of 1922-23, he was captured and in those hardened times, youth was no passport to special treatment. Tortured by his pro-Treaty captors he bore the effects for the rest of his life, never regaining the full use of his right arm. As a politician, Sherwin championed the causes of the poor and dispossessed.

A number of commemorative plaques adorn the Frank Sherwin Bridge: recording its namesake in English and Irish, Phroinsias Uí Shearbháin; the official opening in August 1982 by the Lord Mayor of Dublin, Councillor Dan Browne and the granting of the Irish Concrete Society Award of 1982 to the bridge.

Above: protected by a coffer-dam, workers place concrete on the base rock below the river bed as a foundation for the bridge piers.

Below: the last step – a capstone is placed above a pillar graced with a plaque.

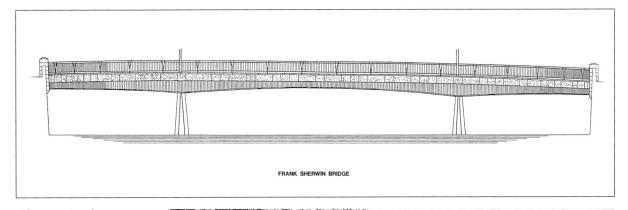

FRANK SHERWIN BRIDGE

Above: a simple structure, consisting of a reinforced concrete beam and slab supported by the abutments and two sets of centre piers.

Right: the coffer dam made up of interlocking sheet-piles, placed in the river to allow the pier foundations to be built.

The Structure

The Frank Sherwin Bridge is a girder type comprising three spans over a 50 metre distance. The centre span is 22 metres and each side span is 14 metres. Cast in situ, the deck is one continuous piece of reinforced concrete and is 20 metres wide.

The bridge piers, arranged in two rows of three, stand on rock foundations in the river and are set back a little from the face of the bridge itself. They were constructed using sheet piled cofferdams. Reinforced concrete abutments are supported on steel-encased concrete piles which were driven to the limestone bedrock. The soft profile of the bridge was achieved by varying the thickness of the deck to curve the soffit or underside, with the maximum depth of any one slab being 0.7 metres. Precast panels of impregnated Scottish and Wicklow granite dust were applied as a finish to the top half of the bridge while on the lower half growth ring boards were employed. Steel parapet railings run along either side, the posts being forked to complement the complex geometric shape of the piers. The bridge designer was Richard Fowler of Dublin Corporation and it was built by Irishenco. The total cost was £1.8 million, or almost €2.3 million. The bridge was officially opened in August 1982.

Below: pumping concrete – the bridge deck is constructed.

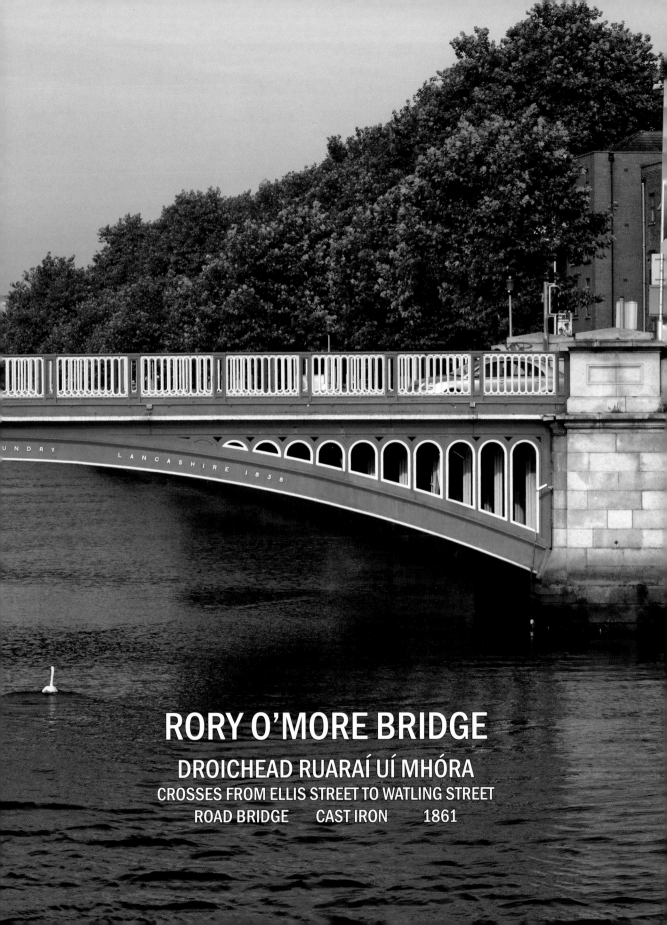

RORY O'MORE BRIDGE

DROICHEAD RUARAÍ UÍ MHÓRA
CROSSES FROM ELLIS STREET TO WATLING STREET
ROAD BRIDGE   CAST IRON   1861

Above: the view from on high. Two lanes of traffic are carried efficiently by this 19th-century cast-iron bridge.

The first crossing of the Rory O'More Bridge was on 29th August 1861 and by no less than the celebrity couple of the day – Queen Victoria and Prince Albert. The occasion was their third visit to Ireland. The royal pair had arrived by train from Killarney where they had spent a few days viewing the wild beauty of the landscape. They traversed the bridge by carriage, thereby declaring it open to all other traffic.

The bridge crosses from Ellis Street on the north bank to Watling Street on the south and is often known simply as the Watling Street Bridge. Its pleasant, flat appearance is due to its low rise – a mere 2.9 metres. It has a single span of 29 metres. The width is 10 metres and the material is cast iron – it also incorporates a wrought-iron deck. The structure was cast at St Helens Foundry in Lancashire, England to the design of the civil engineer, George Halpin Junr, for Dublin Port. On arrival at Dublin, the cast-iron superstructure was sailed upriver to the bridge site. There, massive granite abutments extending three metres from the quay walls had been constructed. Iron cleats were used in attaching the spandrels to the abutments, which, at rib level, are angled for a neat perpendicular fit.

The planning and construction of the bridge was dogged by difficulties and delays. Commissioned by the Ballast Office (home of the Dublin Port and Docks Board), it was to be financed by Dublin Corporation through a levy or tax. Those who lobbied for this new bridge included the growing number of householders on the western fringes of the city. Although a world away in their affluent southside suburbs, the Rathmines and Kingstown Town Commissioners were against it. So incensed were they at the prospect of this unnecessary expenditure of taxpayers' money on a bridge in what was then such an isolated location, that they took the matter to court. They lost and

Right: map of the bridge and area.

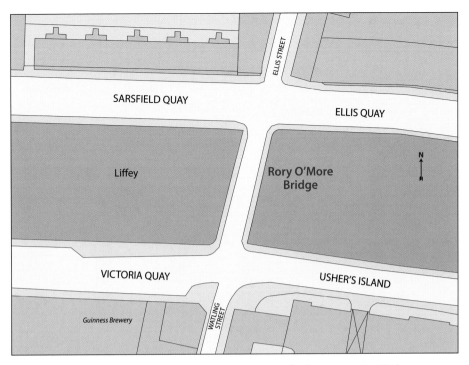

Below: the Eucharistic Congress (one of the largest of the 20th century) was held in Dublin in 1932. The bridge provided a fitting stage for one of the ceremonies.

construction began – the year is recorded on both the upriver and downriver sides of the iron superstructure: Robert Daglish Junr St. Helens Foundry Lancashire, 1858.

However, by the middle of 1860, work at the bridge site had ground to a halt. The contractor blamed difficulties with the foundations. In response Dublin Corporation appointed John Killen of Malahide to complete the job which he did just in time for the royal visit. However, the cost of construction had increased. Budgeted in 1855 at 7,556 guineas the final account was for 11,000 guineas. A glimpse of the adaptability of commercial life in the city in the mid-19th century is provided by a newspaper advertisement of the time. No sooner had Queen Victoria and Prince Albert inaugurated the new bridge than Killen set up his stall on site and offered for sale his now-redundant bridge building equipment: a 10 horse-power steam engine, ladders, wooden pumps and pulley blocks.

The Rory O'More Bridge is the fourth or perhaps even the fifth structure to span the River Liffey at or near this location. The first bridge built here was a simple wooden structure dating from 1671 – this was much needed by the expanding city which was served at the time by just one ancient bridge and sundry ferries that crossed the Liffey. Those championing what was then a building boom on the north river bank had petitioned for the bridge. However some, including aldermen of the corporation who had vested interests in the ferry businesses, conspired to derail the project.

From the moment the first timber pile was driven into the river bed, the structure was attacked by organised gangs of apprentices carrying out the nefarious work of the well-heeled aldermen. Somehow the bridge was finished and opened but in July of that same year the apprentices gathered for one

Above: the four-arch, masonry bridge dating from around 1700. In 1820, the decorative city gate, in mock-Tudor style, on the south of the bridge (then known as 'Bloody Bridge') was built, to a design by Francis Johnston. It was known as the Richmond Tower, after the Viceroy of the time. In 1846 the tower was relocated to the western entrance to the Royal Hospital Kilmainham after the GS&WR built their new station at Kingsbridge, and the tower was considered to be blocking access to the station.

Left: the Richmond Tower today, at Kilmainham.

more assault. The military trooped down from Dublin Castle and a running battle ensued. Twenty young men were seized, first brought to the castle and then marched along the quays en route to prison, accompanied by four files of soldiers. At the new bridge they were ambushed. In the ensuing street battle four were killed and many injured. The prisoners escaped but the bridge did not. It was rebuilt, perhaps twice, and to Dubliners it was, of course, known as the Bloody Bridge.

An unembellished four-arch stone bridge also known as Bloody Bridge was then constructed sometime around 1700. The name Barrack Bridge is also of this vintage – the world's largest military barracks of the time, now known as Collins Barracks, was built on the north-west flank of the bridge from 1701. This new bridge was described by one visitor to Dublin as 'rude' in appearance. There was once a decorative tower with an archway on the south side, designed by Francis Johnston (who designed many prominent buildings in Dublin, including the GPO). In 1846 the tower was removed to the Royal Hospital Kilmainham as it caused an obstruction to traffic heading to the new GS&WR railway station at Kingsbridge. By 1855 this stone bridge, Dublin's oldest at that time, was in a dangerous state with fissures visible, though it was still in use as late as 1858 when there was an affray on it between soldiers of the 30th and 58th regiments when they assaulted each other with sticks, belts and stones.

Today's Rory O'More Bridge has also had a number of different names. Initially it was the Victoria and Albert Bridge or even just the Victoria Bridge. The name was to change again, on the centenary of Catholic Emancipation. Throughout the 18th century and into the 19th Catholics (and Dissenters) in Ireland had suffered discrimination. This had been given legal standing from the time of the first Penal Laws of 1695 when it was decreed that no Catholic could aspire to professional or civic office, buy a decent horse or even practise their religion. Land ownership rights were limited. Repeal had come in 1829, propelled by the efforts of Daniel O'Connell. In 1929 more than a quarter of a million people attended open air mass in the Phoenix Park, in commemoration of Catholic Emancipation, and then marched along the quays to the bridge where the final benediction was given. The bridge was renamed Emancipation Bridge and a commemorative plaque adorns the rise on the east side bridge inscribed: *'1829-1929, Saoirse Creidimh',*beneath which in Latin: *'Anno Centesimo Pas Ivra Politic Maioribvs Nostris Catholicis Reddita IX Kal IVL MCM XXLX Edvardvs Archiep Dublinen Ex Altare Svper Huncpontem Apte Structo Benedixit Cum Ssmo Sacramento Muhitvdinem Ovingenorvm Fere Milivm Fidelivm Adstante Nuntio Sedis speciali Vna Cum Hibernorvm Antistibus Vniversis'.* Symbolically the plaque is engraved with a simple bell, for the time when it was not allowed to ring a Catholic church bell.

The name 'Emancipation', did not last long. In 1939 the bridge was renamed Rory O'More Bridge. O'More, described by a contemporary as 'handsome, courteous and agreeable in nature, a man of courage with a melodious voice', was a 17th-century rebel leader. Born around 1600, he

Below: the bridge has had a multitude of names. In 1939 it was named after the 17th-century rebel chieftain, Rory O'More. The plaque commemorates its previous title of 'Emancipation Bridge' in 1929.

could claim kinship with the Sarsfields, the O'Neills, the Barnewells and the Ormondes. But by the middle of the 17th century the O'Mores had much to feel aggrieved about – the clan were dispossessed of their lands and scattered to the four winds. O'More sowed the seeds of rebellion among his relatives and like-minded friends. The call to arms promised glory, grandeur and the recovery of lost ancestral lands. Despite initial success and the formation of an Irish government – the Catholic Confederation – the rebellion failed and ultimately brought Oliver Cromwell and his 10,000 soldiers to Irish soil in 1649 to snuff out any traces of dissent.

The Rory O'More Bridge was the Liffey's third cast-iron bridge after the Ha'penny Bridge of 1816 and the King's (Seán Heuston) Bridge of 1829. It is also the starting point of one of the most gruelling and unique river races in the world – the Liffey Swim, inaugurated in 1920 from just upstream of the bridge. Today competitors come from all over the world to participate in this event now sponsored by Dublin City Council. Spectators gather to watch along the length of the river but most especially from the Rory O'More Bridge – a timeless and elegant structure now, painted in its characteristic blue, in the very heart of Dublin.

Above: a busy scene from the 1950s, just upriver of the bridge. A locomotive transports Guinness barrels to the quayside, where they are being loaded on barges, destined for cross-channel ships at Dublin Port.

Below: Robert Daglish Junr is commemorated on the cast-iron arch.

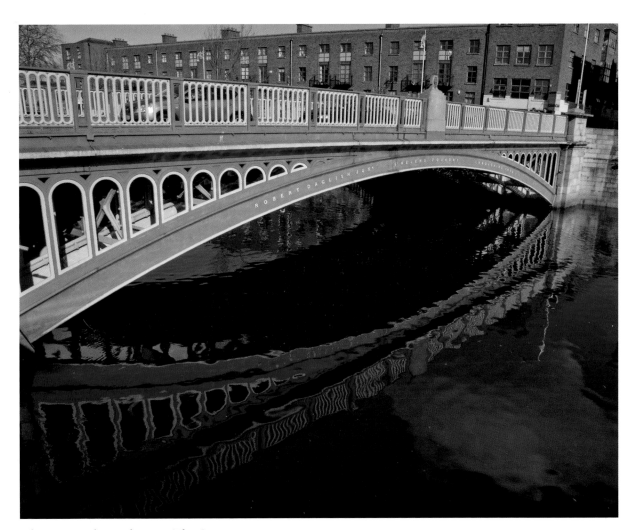

Above: a jewel over the river. The decorated cast iron and arch, as reflected in still Liffey waters.

The Structure

The Rory O'More Bridge is a single arch structure with a span of 29 metres and a width of 10 metres. It carries two lanes of traffic and two footpaths. Seven iron ribs underpin the main bridge framework and these, with the open spandrels away from the crown, directly support the bridge decking. Unusually, the deck itself is of wrought-iron buckled plates and tee irons. The parapet is of cast iron and is in fourteen openwork sections interspaced by rectangular separators. The sections themselves are further divided into ten ellipses. The openwork motif recurs in the iron arch.

The granite abutments protrude over three metres from the quay walls continuing a pattern of well-cut ashlar, though in the case of the abutments with decorative cornices, dadoes and plinths. A variation of the vertical faces of the abutments occurs where the ribs adjoin, being angled so that the ribs sit perpendicular to the masonry.

On both east and west sides the arch ring is inscribed 'Robert Daglish Junr. St. Helens Foundry Lancashire 1858'. The designer was George Halpin of the Dublin Port and Docks Board and the contractor John Killen.

The Rory O'More Bridge opened in 1861 at a cost of 11,000 guineas or almost €17,000.

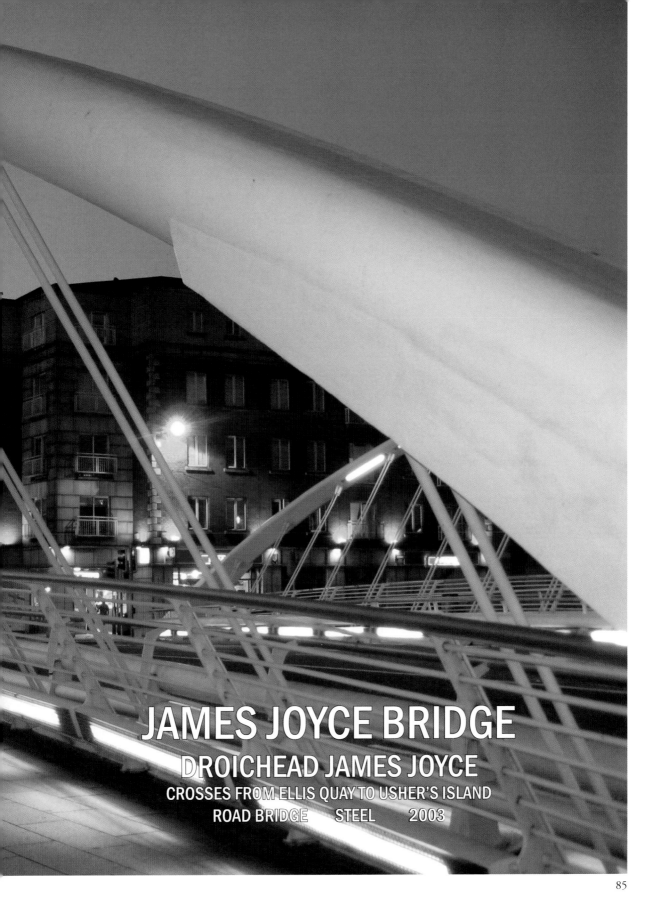

JAMES JOYCE BRIDGE
DROICHEAD JAMES JOYCE
CROSSES FROM ELLIS QUAY TO USHER'S ISLAND
ROAD BRIDGE   STEEL   2003

In tribute to its namesake, the James Joyce Bridge was officially opened on 16th June 2003, a date popularly known as Bloomsday. The bridge is in the tradition of Liffey bridges being arched – it has two outward-angled arches supporting the deck. Its neighbours too are arched: Mellows, the oldest existing crossing, to the east and the cast-iron, Victorian Rory O'More Bridge to the west. Yet, designer Santiago Calatrava's daring signature white, steel and concrete, single-span structure, his first for the city of Dublin, manages to defy convention. It is arched but it is unlike anything that went before. James Joyce, the iconoclast, would have approved.

Conceptually the bridge design differs too. Pedestrians are not merely consigned to a footpath appended on to the traffic lanes, but are given clearly defined spaces on both the upstream and downstream sides: passageways protected by an overhanging arch which is angled outwards at 20 degrees from the deck. The pathways curve, varying in width from three to six metres and the floors are transparent. The parapets mirror the curving walkways and are of toughened glass, cleanly trimmed with stainless steel. Stone seating is provided to encourage leisurely use of the bridge.

The James Joyce Bridge carries four lanes of vehicular traffic. Its concrete composite slab deck rests on a grillage of structural steel members and is suspended from the curved ribs by 32 pairs of high tensile steel rods. The ribs reach a height of 8.5 metres above the general level of the deck, whose width between railings is 30 metres. The total span is 40 metres. Beneath the superstructure, piles in the river and adjacent to the quay walls provide additional support, while the abutments are integrated into the quay walls.

Below: James Joyce, iconoclast and genius, who wrote what is regarded as the most outstanding novel of the 20th century, 'Ulysses'. This fine statue at North Earl Street, Dublin, is by Marjorie Fitzgibbon.

Right: map of the bridge area.

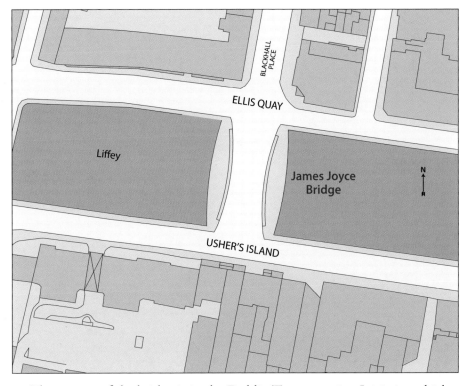

Below: genius at work – Santiago Calatrava, from Valencia in Spain. An engineer and architect, he has designed many innovative bridges and buildings around the world in his distinctive style. His vision, it is said, is one of bridging the division between structural engineering and architecture.

The genesis of the bridge is in the Dublin Transportation Initiative which in 1995 recommended the planning of environmental traffic cells to bring greater fluency to traffic movement in the city with the additional benefit of establishing a more pleasant city experience for the pedestrian and cyclist. The study envisaged two new bridges: one each, east and west of that reliable old work horse across the river, O'Connell Bridge. Thus the James Joyce Bridge was conceptually twinned from the outset with what was to be Calatrava's second Dublin bridge, the Samuel Beckett.

In the case of the James Joyce Bridge there was a local context too: the area around Blackhall Place was, in the closing years of the 20th century, socially deprived and commercially stagnant. In 1996, Dublin Corporation published a framework for an Historic Area Rejuvenation Project in which a new bridge was also central.

An Environmental Impact Statement of 1998 put three bridge types under the spotlight – single span, long single span and a three span. The quays were a busy arterial route through the city – the Port Tunnel was not yet built – but preserving the dynamic visual pattern with views of the Four Courts and the existing bridges was paramount. The site, near the heart of the old city, was important and warranted a bridge of significant aesthetic merit. Some visual obstruction was unavoidable but the light and transparent bridge design, eventually decided upon, minimised this.

Santiago Calatrava, engineer and architect, was appointed in 1998. In 1999 he submitted his proposal for the bridge and a supplementary environmental impact study was undertaken to consider the impact of this specific design.

In March 2001 building commenced on the structure which had the working title of 'Blackhall Place Bridge'. During construction the river itself became the workplace and site deliveries were at off peak times thus keeping disruption of road traffic to a minimum. A temporary bridge was constructed to support the deck, which was fabricated off site and assembled in situ. When ready it was incrementally lowered using computer-controlled hydraulic jacks so that the correct deflection of the bridge was achieved. It was originally planned to be a manual exercise but the risk to the jack operatives, who would be under the structure during the load transfer, was deemed too great. Precision too was at issue – the deck was lowered at fourteen differential rates – an electronically guided operation offered the required control.

The supporting arches, fabricated off site at Harland and Wolff, Belfast, were assembled by welding on the temporary deck. On the 13th and 19th

Above: the first of the Calatrava-designed bridges in Dublin, the James Joyce Bridge has a distinct luminosity at night.

October 2002 these were lowered into place also using the computer-monitored precision system.

Actual construction time was 26 months, six months longer than initially planned. Factors in the delay included: piling complexities arising from a buried river; the challenging nature of the river bed here at one of the narrowest points of the Liffey within the city; welding complexities with the steel fabrication and the flooding of the working platform twice a day by the tides. The completed cost was €9 million.

The bridge's name is apt – the area has Joycean connections (designer Calatrava is also a Joycean scholar). Joyce's short story *The Dead* was set in the fictional Kate and Julia Morkan's house at 15 Usher's Island, now a fitting southside backdrop for the bridge. On the north side, the lawyers at the nearby Law Society at Blackhall Place (previously the Blue Coat School) bore the brunt of some of Ulysses' anti-hero, Leopold Bloom's ire.

Below: what lies beneath – work underway on piling to a secure sub-base to achieve a solid foundation.

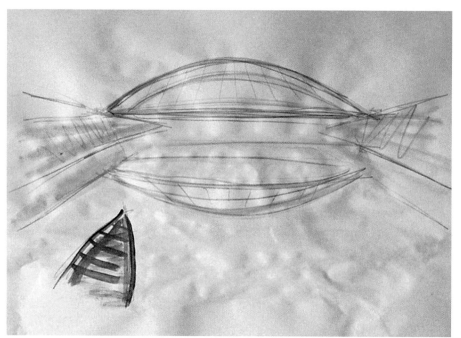

Joyce wrote his only known children's story about a bridge in 1936: *The Cat and the Devil*. Written in a letter to his grandson Stevie, the story centres on the town of Beaugency, whose people longed for a bridge but had no money to build one. Their Lord Mayor was a fictional Alfred Byrne, the real one being Lord Mayor of Dublin from 1930 to 1939. Cunningly he outwits the devil who is rumoured to speak bad French with a Dublin accent.

James Joyce was a Dubliner and from a young age an intimate of the city, in seeming incessant movement with his middle-class family, ever leaving one address for a less salubrious other. They traversed the city, from leafy Rathgar to Blackrock by the sea; from exile in Bray, Co. Wicklow to northside anonymity in Fairview. The imprudent ways and alcoholism of Joyce's father, John Stanislaus, propelled their humiliating descent into poverty. From a young age, Joyce attended schools and later university in the city.

Joyce took his first literary footsteps at the tender age of nine, writing an ode to Charles Stewart Parnell, a nationalist hero of his father. By the time he was studying at University College, Dublin, he was part of an eclectic artistic circle within the city. While writing, Joyce worked as a singer, reviewer, newspaper proprietor, translator, sub-editor, teacher, lecturer, cinema impresario and journalist. Like his father he nurtured a fondness for alcohol and like his mother he sometimes relied on the kindness of others for his family's daily bread.

Wanderlust and necessity saw Joyce set up home in Rome, Zurich, Trieste, Pula and Paris – anywhere but Dublin. Yet, Dublin was the novelist's setting of choice and his characters are Dubliners – and Anna Livia Plurabelle, the River Liffey.

A plaque on the James Joyce Bridge commemorates the official opening by the Lord Mayor of Dublin, Dermot Lacey.

The bridge faces no. 15 Usher's Island, below. James Joyce wrote his finest short story 'The Dead' centered around a fictional social gathering here.

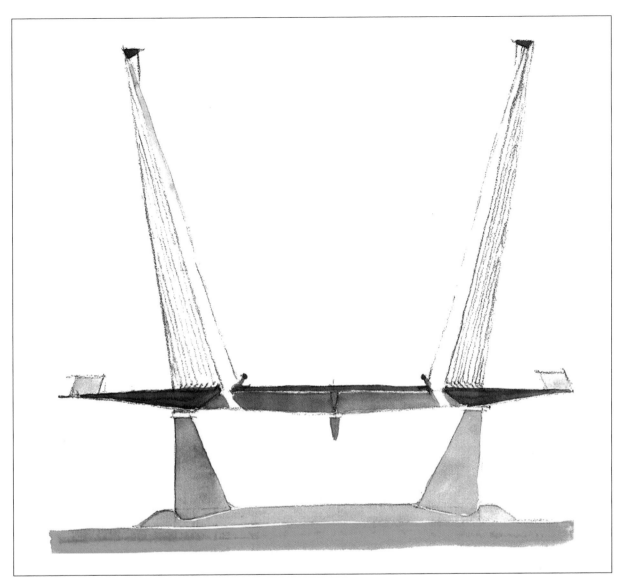

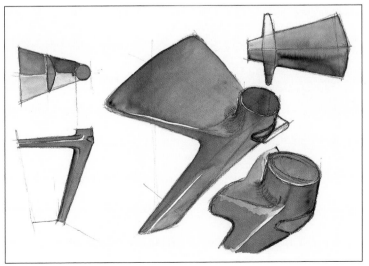

Raw steel was fabricated
at Harland and Wolff's
premises in Belfast, above.
Millimetre by millimetre,
it was painstakingly assembled on site, above right.
Geometric and white,
the completed bridge now
graces the Dublin quays,
left.

Below: Michael Phillips,
Dublin City Engineer at
the opening of the bridge.

The Structure

The James Joyce Bridge is a tied-arch structure. The deck is supported from two outward-angled arches. High-tensile steel rods, 32 in total, hang from each arch down to the deck. Piles in the river and at the quay walls provide support for the overall structure. Its single span is 40 metres and the deck width between railings is 30 metres.

The bridge connects Ellis Quay on the north bank of the Liffey to Usher's Island on the south with two-way vehicular traffic being accommodated in four lanes. Pedestrian walkways on either side are cantilevered from the deck on the outside and are supported by angled stringers between the deck and arches which create a physical barrier between pedestrians and traffic. The width of the curved walkways varies from three to six metres and the overhanging arches are inclined outwards at 20 degrees. The bridge parapets are of glass and it is one of only three Liffey bridges with seating for pedestrians, the others being Grattan Bridge and Rosie Hackett Bridge. Both abutments are integrated into the existing quay walls. Recessed lighting along with that above head height on the arches illuminate the bridge at night.

Construction began in March 2001 to a design by Santiago Calatrava. Irishenco Ltd was the main contractor and Roughan O'Donovan the engineers. The superstructure was fabricated in Belfast by Harland and Wolff. A temporary deck in the river facilitated assembly. Completion of the bridge took 26 months. The bridge opened on Bloomsday, 16th June 2003.

MELLOWS BRIDGE

DROICHEAD UÍ MHAOILÍOSA

CROSSES FROM QUEEN STREET TO BRIDGEFOOT STREET

ROAD BRIDGE   MASONRY ARCH   1768

Mellows Bridge connects Queen Street on the north bank to Bridgefoot Street on the south. It is the most senior of the Liffey bridges within the city and was built before even Richmond Bridge – the oldest along the Thames in London. It has provided Dubliners with a road and pedestrian crossing at this point since 1768.

Construction of the bridge began in 1764 to a design by the engineer Charles Vallancey who settled in Ireland, having arrived to assist in a military survey. Surviving drawings show that the foundations of the piers were laid in caissons or open-topped, watertight boxes, usually of timber, which were fixed on the river bed and gradually sunk by continuously digging out material from within. The masonry of the piers is smoothly rusticated, emphasising the block shape. Each pier is topped by a capstone above which is a recess or nook which may have housed statuary in the past.

Most likely the semi-circular arches of the bridge were constructed using support from wooden frames, a common technique known as timber centring. The haunches, or those parts of the arch on either side of the crown, extend to the quarter points of the arches and are of stone construction with a clay fill.

The masonry is evenly-coursed granite ashlar, that is blocks of uniform size laid in a regular horizontal pattern. Voussoirs, or wedge shaped stones, alternating large and small, mark out each arch. The larger voussoirs are vermiculated – sculpted with asymmetric wave patterns similar to worm tracks. The others have simple roll mouldings.

Above: the semi-circular arches of Mellows Bridge span the river. This is the oldest of the Liffey bridges.

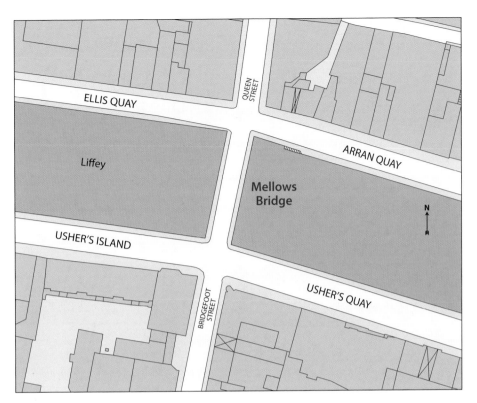

Right: map of the bridge area.

The abutments at the quay walls slope outwards and are part of the arch support. The overall height of the parapet at the rise of the bridge from top to base is 1.6 metres. The coping is supported by the cast-iron balusters or pillars, interspaced with dadoes which in turn rest on two layers of masonry, the lower one serving as a plinth.

When first opened, the bridge was named for Queen Charlotte, wife of George III, king of Great Britain and Ireland. Known as the Queen's Bridge, it was a tribute to a popular royal who, as a 17 year old plucked from her aristocratic German home, first met her husband on the morning of their wedding. Refurbishment of the Queen's Bridge took place in 1818, the year of Queen Charlotte's death. It was at that time that the parapets were replaced by those we see today.

The Queen's Bridge was the second structure on this site. The first was the Arran Bridge of 1683. Dublin was then experiencing a property boom (it was ever thus!). There was a flurry of land speculation and building taking place on the north bank of the river, which up until then had been largely undeveloped. Although London had rapidly grown when Charles II was restored to the throne in 1660, it took the arrival of James Butler, Duke of Ormonde to waken Dublin from its medieval slumber. The city was a maze of meandering, narrow streets and lanes lined with run-down houses, shops and taverns. The population had declined and the city could boast of only one bridge.

Between 1670 and 1683 four new bridges were built over the River Liffey – the Arran Bridge here being the last of these. Most importantly, Ormonde had decreed that buildings should no longer back onto the Liffey (they also

had conveniently emptied their everyday waste into it), but should face the river. A William Ellis was granted land on the shoreline of the north side of the river and struck a deal with the city authorities: he would build quaysides, a bridge and look after its maintenance, they would contribute £700. Astutely, Ellis named the bridge for his friend, Richard, Earl of Arran and fourth son of the Duke of Ormonde. Richard, who purchased the Aran Islands while still a young man, equally astutely had made a fortune from the making and issuing of farthing and halfpence coins for Ireland.

The ravages of time, poor construction quality and a ferocious flood brought the four-arch Arran Bridge down in 1763. In the intervening years Dublin had blossomed with new, elegant squares and wide avenues. The population had grown from around a meagre 50,000 to over 120,000. The north side of the river was now a lively commercial and residential hub and it was essential that the Arran Bridge be replaced with all speed.

Above: a scene from yesteryear. Guinness barges sail through an arch of Mellows Bridge. There is clearance here, but to cope with bridges that had low clearance at high tide, the barges had a hinge on the funnel.

Right: detail was everything in this 18th-century bridge. Fine masonry on this well-crafted round-headed niche, over the cut-water at a pier in the river. The vermiculation on the voussoirs can be seen – this comprises of asymmetric wave patterns similar to worm tracks.

Below: plaque to Liam Mellows on the bridge.

No known records exist of why it took almost four years, from 1764 to 1768, to construct the new bridge – perhaps there was more attention paid to the quality of the construction. Perhaps, as was not uncommon in those days, it was a mixture of corruption, disreputable builders, together with a reluctance on the part of the city authorities to part with taxes and of citizens to pay them.

However, the Queen's Bridge served the city well, being renamed Queen Maeve's Bridge in 1922. Maeve was a mythological queen of Connaught who stole the Brown Bull of Cooley. The aldermen of Dublin chose her name, during the great rebranding of the colonially-named streets, bridges and buildings of Dublin after Ireland gained independence.

In December of that same year, 1922, Liam Mellows was executed by firing squad in Mountjoy Jail. It was an act of reprisal in the course of the bitter Irish Civil War, the sides being divided on the question of the Anglo-Irish

Treaty, which granted dominion status to 26 Irish counties, not the desired Republic. Mellows was anti-Treaty, having been captured in the previous June following the fall of the Four Courts. He was one of four men shot without trial, each one representing a province of Ireland, in the immediate aftermath of the assassination of a pro-Treaty TD. Liam Mellows was considered to represent Connaught.

Mellows was a veteran of the nationalist struggle. In 1916 he had been jailed for his nationalist activities, then escaped back to Galway to take part in the Easter Rising. From there he went to the United States. He returned to Ireland in 1920 and was elected to Dáil Eireann in 1921. Queen Maeve's Bridge became Mellows Bridge in 1942.

Brass commemorative plaques, one each on the upstream and downstream sides of the bridge, read: "The name of this bridge has been changed to Mellows Bridge to honour the memory of Lieut-General Liam Mellows, Irish Republican Army, who gave his life for the Republic of Ireland, 8th December 1922. Erected by the National Graves Association". The plaques were unveiled in the presence of Liam Mellows' mother, Sarah.

Below: the leader of the Volunteers in 1916 Galway, Liam Mellows was prominent in the anti-Treaty forces in the Four Courts in June 1922. He was executed, without trial, in December of that year.

Bridge, Dublin.

Above: Charles Vallancey's bridge, dating from 1768. It has a classical design and gives an impression of perfect harmony.

The Structure

Mellows Bridge is a three-arch, stone structure with a span of 43 metres. The arches are semi-circular in shape. The masonry is evenly coursed granite ashlar. On the arch rings and piers the masonry is rusticated or roughened. The arch rings are defined by a series of voussoirs sculpted in irregular waves. These alternate with smaller stones decorated with roll mouldings. The bridge piers are triangular in plan with smoothly rusticated masonry and are each crowned with a large capstone, which functions as a cutwater resisting the flow of water on the bridge structure. Decorative round-headed niches top the capstones.

The parapet is made up of cast-iron balusters, nine series in all, interspaced with dadoes and capped with coping stones. There are two larger dadoes on both the east and west sides with those on the rise of the bridge bearing commemorative plaques. Beneath the balustrades there are two ashlar masonry courses, the bottom one of which serves as a plinth. The bridge has the most severe gradient of all Liffey bridges.

Mellows Bridge was completed in 1768 to a design by Charles Vallancey.

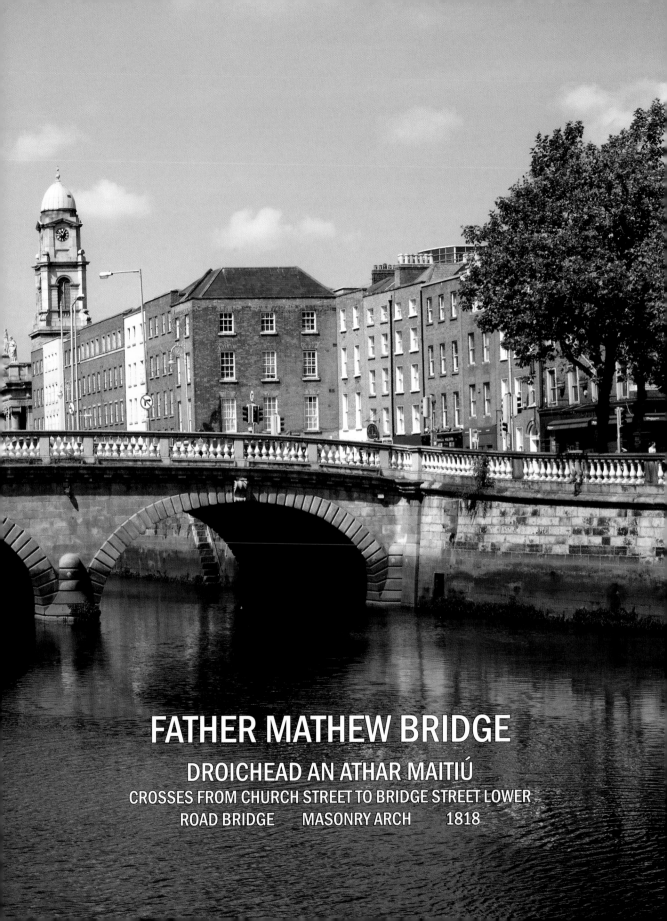

FATHER MATHEW BRIDGE

DROICHEAD AN ATHAR MAITIÚ
CROSSES FROM CHURCH STREET TO BRIDGE STREET LOWER
ROAD BRIDGE   MASONRY ARCH   1818

Father Mathew Bridge crosses the River Liffey from Church Street on the north bank to the aptly named Bridge Street on the south. It is on the site of the oldest known Liffey crossing which dates back over 1,000 years. The bridge, along with Mellows Bridge of 1768 to the west, and O'Donovan Rossa Bridge of 1816 just 220 metres away to the east, forms part of an elegant and historic bridge trio at the heart of the old city.

Above: the site of the first Liffey crossing point; Father Mathew Bridge from the air.

Construction of the Father Mathew Bridge began in 1816. Designer George Knowles based his blueprints on those of James Savage for the Richmond (O'Donovan Rossa) Bridge on which Knowles had also worked and which opened in 1816. A proposal to build a single-span bridge was rejected as being aesthetically unacceptable – the beauty and character of the three-span structure could not be 'entirely lost'.

The contract price at £25,800 which included 'clearing for foundations which are to be laid on solid rock' was the same as that for Savage's bridge. In keeping with the form established by the adjacent bridges, this structure is a three-arch masonry bridge with a parapet of cast-iron balusters, the series interrupted by masonry dadoes, topped by coping stones and underlain by a stone plinth. Voussoirs, or wedge shaped stones, decorate the arch ring with off-centre keystones on each arch. The masonry work, too, is similar across these three singular Liffey bridges. The stone is granite, cut in evenly shaped blocks of consistent height and laid horizontally. On the piers, arch rings and arch soffits, it is smoothly rusticated, the recessed joints giving definition to each block. The span is 45 metres, the same as the O'Donovan Rossa and two metres more than the older Mellows Bridge.

Right: plan of the bridge area.

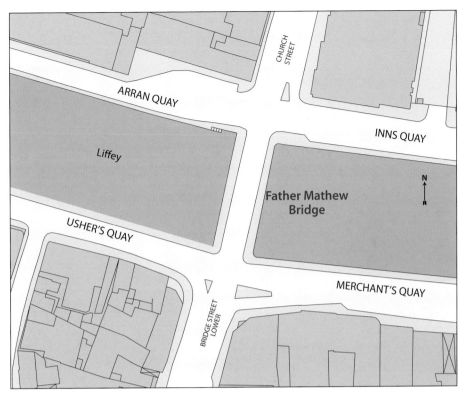

Below: Father Mathew, (1790–1856) the noted temperance reformer, administring the temperance pledge, by the Custom House. Tipperary-born, this Capuchin priest formed an abstinence movement which was very successful both in Ireland and abroad.

Construction methods were of the time. Wooden frames were used to provide support for the construction of the arches – this was known as timber centring. Most likely caissons – timber, watertight boxes open on top which were gradually sunk into the riverbed by excavating from within – were used to build the foundations. There was a cost overrun (not uncommon on bridges over the Liffey down the ages!), the final bill amounted to £26,000.

The site is an historic one and crossings of the River Liffey here have had a confusion of guises and names. Dublin's earliest settlers built a ford here to move between their settlement on the muddy southside banks to the fields and swamp lands on the opposite bank through which routes to the north of the country ran. When the Vikings invaded and established a settlement they built their own bridge here, a timber frame structure, known as Dubhghalls' Bridge. It was on this bridge that nine warriors fleeing from the Battle of Clontarf in 1014 met their bloody end.

In 1180 the death of Lawrence O'Toole, Archbishop of Dublin, in far-off Normandy was recorded as resulting from the effects of an earlier fall from the 'Dublin Bridge', most likely this same wooden bridge.

The Norman King John gave his royal assent to a new bridge for Dublin in 1214. It was of stone and timber construction and became known as King John's Bridge. Nevertheless, scribes around 1240 were still referring to the 'Ostman's Bridge'. Ostmen were the Norse (Danish) settlers in Ireland. By all accounts the bridge had shops and houses, protected by a tower and accessed through a bridge gate. When in 1317 Edward Bruce, brother of Scotland's King Robert, threatened Dublin, the citizens tore the bridge down, used the

stone to fortify the city walls and, when the threat had passed, rebuilt the bridge.

Liffey floods, notorious for their ferocity and unpredictable nature, washed away this bridge in 1385. Construction of a replacement did not begin for another 40 years and was financed by the tolls from ferries which plied the Liffey.

As was customary in medieval times, the care of the new bridge, completed in 1428, was entrusted to a religious order, the Dominicans, who exacted a toll for its use and in return bestowed blessings of holy water. Travellers called it the Friars' Bridge. An inelegant structure of four unequal stone arches, it served the expanding city through almost 400 years. In 1670 another bridge, the Bloody Bridge, was built over the river, the city's second. The original bridge here then became known as the Old Bridge.

By 1814 the bridge was a 'crazy, wretched pile of antiquity' but still in everyday use. George Knowles was asked to tender for a new bridge in 1815 and construction commenced the following year.

Upon opening the new bridge was named for Charles, Earl of Whitworth, Irish Viceroy from 1813 to 1817. A diplomat and impoverished eldest son, he was a favourite of queens, duchesses and countesses to whom he was a generous purveyor of flattery and friendship. They, in turn, discreetly replenished

Above: a centuries-old oil painting of the bridge by the Four Courts.

Below: plaque to Father Mathew, after whom the bridge was named in 1938. This is the latest of many names here, which ranged from: 'Old Bridge'; 'Whitworth Bridge' and 'Dublin Bridge'.

his ever-empty purse. When in time he married an heiress, Diana Arabella, it was through her influence he gained the appointment of Viceroy.

In 1922 the Whitworth Bridge became simply Dublin Bridge, though this name was short-lived. In 1938 it was renamed Father Mathew Bridge in honour of the Tipperary-born priest who in the mid-19th century had brought hope to Dublin's poor. A contemporary of Daniel O'Connell, the pair wrought great changes on the Irish social and political landscape. While O'Connell led the people towards emancipation and the gradual achievement of political power, Father Mathew dealt with the destructiveness of alcoholism on Irish society. His Irish Total Abstinence Society instituted 'the pledge' – a promise to abstain from alcohol. Six million people, nationally and internationally, made this promise, including Pope Gregory XVI and the escaped slave and social reformer Frederick Douglass who, when on a visit to Ireland was personally initiated by Father Mathew. In 1840 more than 72,000 Dubliners gathered at the Custom House to 'take the pledge'.

Many decades later, in the 1930s, Dubliners were reminded of Father Mathew's crusade when one of their own, Matt Talbot, a reformed alcoholic, died on a Dublin street. In the spirit of those times the bridge was renamed the Father Mathew Bridge.

Today the bridge is used by both road vehicles and pedestrians. The larger dadoes, which are slightly off centre of the rise of the bridge, bear commemorative brass plaques.

FOUR COURTS DUBLIN. 1651.W.L.

Above: a circa 1914 view upriver, including the trio of historic bridges. In the foreground is the O'Donovan Rossa, next is the Father Mathew (both with elliptical arches). The Mellows (with semi-circular arches) can be seen in the misty background.

Left: a view downriver to Father Mathew Bridge through the balustrades of Mellows Bridge. St Paul's of Arran Quay is visible to the left.

The Structure

The Father Mathew Bridge is a three-arch masonry bridge with a span of 45 metres. The arches are elliptical in shape and the centre arch is slightly smaller than the outer two.

The masonry is evenly coursed granite ashlar with that of the arch rings, piers and arch soffits being smoothly rusticated or roughened, the recessed joints emphasising the block shape. No known records exist which describe the type of foundations though the contract included 'clearing for foundations which are to be laid on solid rock'.

Voussoirs define the arch ring, each of which has a decorative keystone which is slightly off centre. Haunching is probably of rubble material with a fill of soft clay. Settlement of around 150 mm in the case of the south pier has been noted.

The parapet, resting on a moulded stone plinth, is of cast-iron balusters, irregularly interspaced with dadoes, a larger dado being marginally off centre at the rise of the bridge on both the east and the west sides. Coping stones, curvilinear in section, top the balusters.

Father Mathew Bridge was completed in 1818 to a design by George Knowles for the Port of Dublin.

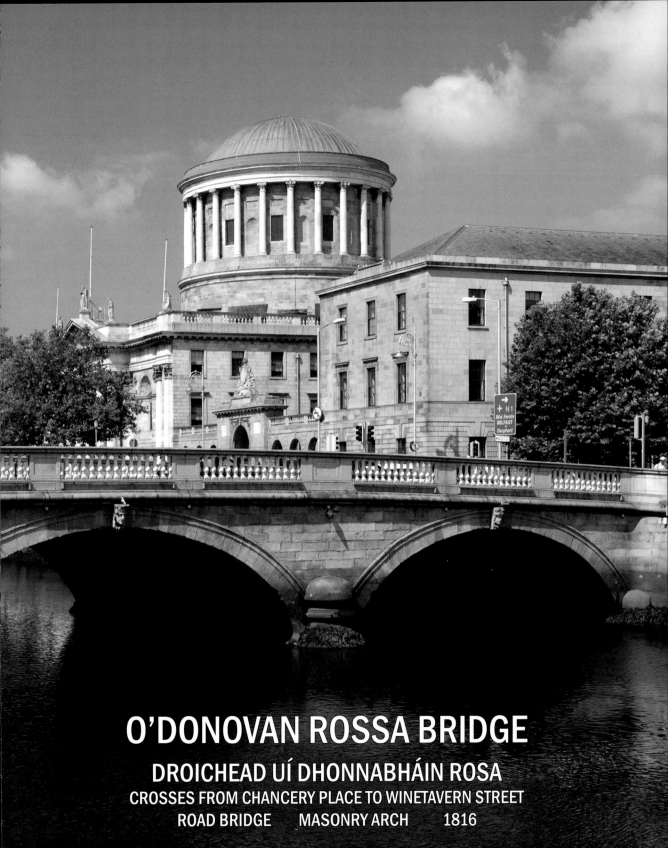

O'DONOVAN ROSSA BRIDGE

DROICHEAD UÍ DHONNABHÁIN ROSA

CROSSES FROM CHANCERY PLACE TO WINETAVERN STREET

ROAD BRIDGE   MASONRY ARCH   1816

Travelling eastwards along the Liffey, O'Donovan Rossa is the last of Dublin's historic trio of masonry bridges, the other two being the Father Mathew Bridge of 1818 and the city's oldest, the Mellows Bridge of 1768. The O'Donovan Rossa Bridge provides a road and pedestrian crossing from Chancery Place on the north bank of the Liffey to Winetavern Street on the south.

Construction began in 1813. Charlotte, the dowager Duchess of Richmond, accompanied by a ceremonial guard and to the sound of two military bands, placed the foundation stone. The project involved a another trio, that of great names in the history of Dublin bridge building – James Savage, later a designer of Gothic churches, George Knowles, a fellow Englishman who also designed and built Lucan Bridge and George Halpin, overseer and Lighthouse Inspector.

O'Donovan Rossa Bridge is a three-arch structure built of Golden Hill, West Wicklow granite, squared and evenly coursed. The span is 45 metres and the width, at just under 16 metres, was greater than any bridge in London at that time. The correspondence of George Knowles tells us that the foundations were laid on solid rock but nothing else is known of their construction. Interestingly, in sinking the foundations several coins from the Elizabethan era were found, along with two boats, one occupied by a human skeleton.

The east and west faces of the bridge are identical though the arch rings, defined by rectangular voussoirs, are each adorned by individual, sculpted Portland stone keystones by the sculptor John Smyth. Gazing westwards from their arch centre point are Commerce, Hibernia and Peace, while Plenty,

Below: the bridge is named after Jeremiah O'Donovan Rossa (1831-1915). From Rosscarbery in West Cork, he was a prominent Fenian and member of the Irish Republican Brotherhood. Pádraig Pearse delivered an electrifying oration at his funeral in 1915.

Right: map of bridge.

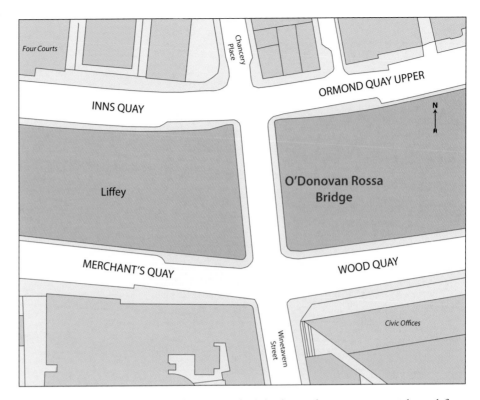

Overleaf: an early 19th-century engraving of the bridges by the Four Courts, with the Richmond (now O'Donovan Rossa) Bridge centre stage. The (then) Essex Bridge and Ha'penny Bridge can be seen in the background.

Anna Livia and Industry look eastwards. The haunching, or material used for that part of the arch between its springing and its crown, is good rubble, most likely recycled from the previous structure, the Ormonde Bridge.

The bridge parapets, in common with that of Father Mathew, Mellows and Lucan Bridges are of cast-iron balusters standing between coping stones and plinth. The balusters are laid in series or groupings, 13 in each group and are interspaced with dadoes – 10 on each side, two small flanked by two larger. That baluster-dado design is also used along the north quay walls, continuing westwards to Father Mathew Bridge. Eight cast-iron lamp standards, four on either side, enhanced the bridge when first built – but were subsequently removed.

The O'Donovan Rossa Bridge is not the first on this site. The first here was the Ormonde Bridge erected in the 17th century. This timber structure was tall enough for ships to pass under, but was constructed without a parapet. The cost of £502 19s 7d was borne by developer and Lord Mayor of Dublin at that time, Sir Humphrey Jervis. Railings were added at a later stage at a cost of £14 which was borne by the city sheriff who, in return, was awarded the licence for the apple stall beside the bridge. Contemporary reports tell us that the railings were repeatedly stolen.

The Ormonde Bridge was built in 1682 after the medieval city on the south bank of the Liffey had rapidly expanded. There was much development at this time along the north quays – within two years the city corporation replaced this timber bridge by a four-arch stone bridge with a wooden drawbridge section. The name Ormonde Bridge was retained. The drawbridge, the

operation of which was the responsibility of the apple stall proprietor, was replaced by a fifth masonry arch in 1685.

Both bridges were named for James Butler, 1st Duke of Ormonde (1610-1688), who could trace his lineage back to the time of Strongbow. As Lord Lieutenant or Viceroy of Ireland he oversaw much change in Dublin, including the building of bridges, the Royal Hospital in Kilmainham and the expansion of the Phoenix Park.

The second Ormonde Bridge served Dubliners for 118 years though in various states of repair. In 1687 it was reported to be in a ruinous state having been damaged by floods. The great George Semple repaired the foundations in 1752. Another spectacular flood in 1760 swept part of the south arch and deck of the bridge, along with Mrs Archer's quayside tavern, complete with customers, into the raging Liffey. Declared 'ready to fall' in 1776, it somehow survived to 1802 when torrential rain caused a 'great body of water' to sweep downriver and wash away the bridge.

Ferries shuttled across this stretch of Liffey water while the corporation planned for a new bridge. A design competition was won by James Savage in 1805 and when construction finally began in 1813 – to Savage's somewhat altered design and around 50 metres from the original site – a temporary, tolled, timber bridge was erected.

Above: the earlier Ormonde Bridge, in 1801, in obvious poor condition. A busy fruit market is underway on the south bank, with the group of buildings known as Pudding Row, in the left background.

116

A SOUTH VIEW ON THE RIVER LIFFEY, DUBLIN.

Above: the same scene, several years on. In the foreground, are what remains of the earlier Ormonde Bridge. It collapsed in 1802, swept away by 'a great body of water'. The Ballast Board decided to construct a replacement stone bridge. The new bridge was named for the Duke of Richmond, then Viceroy.

On St Patrick's Day, 1816 the new bridge was declared open and named Richmond Bridge for yet another Irish Viceroy, Charles Lennox, 4th Duke of Richmond (1764-1819).

According to lore, the duke arrived into this world at an inconvenient time and he was thus born in the nearest shelter, a Scottish barn. After a career as a soldier and parliamentarian he arrived in Dublin in 1807. His time was marked by a glamorous social life for the capital's well-heeled but there was political stagnation after the Act of Union. He died in 1819 while serving as Governor General of British North America. He contracted rabies while on tour and departed this world much as he arrived – in a barn near Richmond, Ontario.

When Richmond Bridge opened the orderly Dublin quayscape visible today had not yet evolved. Access to the bridge from Winetavern Street was rendered narrow by a large group of buildings known as 'Pudding Row' which overhung the bridge at the western end. These were removed in 1820.

This historic bridge served Dubliners well and in 1922, Dublin Corporation renamed it for the great Fenian, Jeremiah O'Donovan Rossa (1831-1915). This was part of the significant renaming exercise that took place in Dublin, capital of the newly independent nation, when colonial-era names on streets and bridges were replaced by those of nationalist heroes.

The bridge is graced by six carved heads, three on each side, at the arch keystones. They are by the noted sculptor John Smyth. Below: a night-time view of the heads on one side of the bridge.

O'Donovan Rossa, from West Cork, had lost family members during the Great Famine but found a cause in nationalism. A member of the Irish Republican Brotherhood, he was arrested, charged with treason and sentenced to life imprisonment in 1865. He was 34, had a growing family and, having already buried two wives, he had married 18 year-old Mary Jane Irwin only a year before. When released in 1871 he sailed for New York where he resumed his revolutionary republican work. He is best known for the dynamite campaign of the 1880s which targeted military and government facilities in Great Britain, being directed by the Fenians in the United States.

When in 1891 he was released from his edict of banishment, O'Donovan Rossa made two last visits home. After he died in New York in August 1915, his body was returned to Ireland. Pádraig Pearse gave an electrifying graveside oration at Glasnevin Cemetery which included the immortal words: 'Ireland unfree shall never be at peace'.

Right: silhouetted by the evening sun, the O'Donovan Rossa Bridge and the Four Courts, in a 1966 photograph.

The Structure

O'Donovan Rossa Bridge is a three-arch, masonry structure with a span of 45 metres. The arches are elliptical in shape. The masonry is evenly coursed granite ashlar with the arch rings, piers and arch soffits being smoothly rusticated or roughened. The foundations rest on solid rock.

Each arch ring is defined by a decorative masonry roll below which are rectangular voussoirs. On both east and west sides sculpted keystone heads rest at the centre point of each arch. Facing eastwards are: Plenty; Anna Livia and Industry. On the western side are: Commerce; Hibernia and Peace.

Haunching is of good rubble material while the fill is compacted clay type material. The haunching extends to the quarter points. On both faces of the bridge the piers are equipped with cutwaters. Each parapet rests on a moulded stone plinth and rises to a height of 1.35 metres at the centre point of the bridge. Cast-iron balusters, arranged in series, interspaced with dadoes, are topped with coping stones and the baluster design continues west along the parapet by Inns Quay to Father Mathew Bridge. Plaques to O'Donovan Rossa were unveiled on the bridge in August 2015.

James Savage, George Knowles and George Halpin collaborated on the construction of this bridge. Savage was described as 'designer', Knowles as 'contractor' and Halpin as 'overseer'. The cost was £25,950. Construction began in 1813 and the bridge opened in 1816.

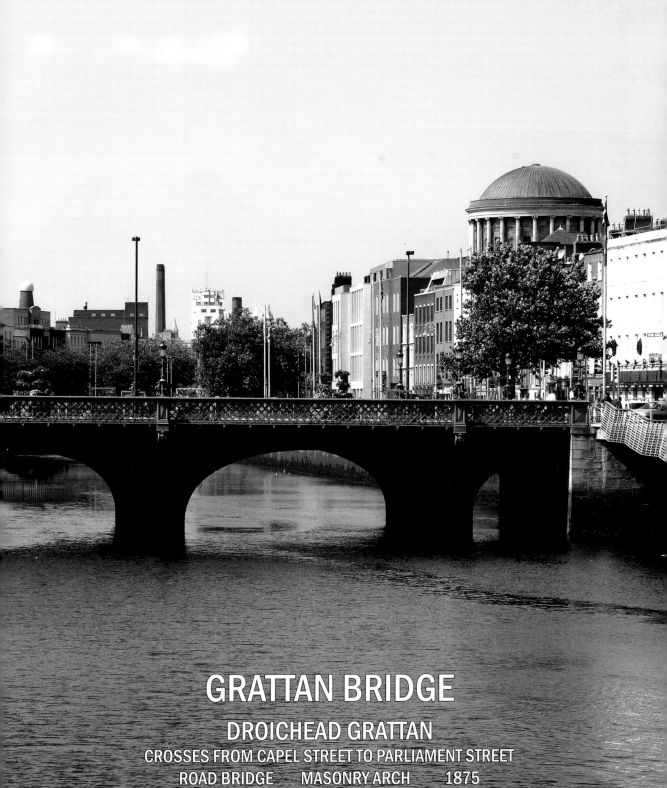

GRATTAN BRIDGE

DROICHEAD GRATTAN
CROSSES FROM CAPEL STREET TO PARLIAMENT STREET
ROAD BRIDGE   MASONRY ARCH   1875

Left: Grattan Bridge from the air.

O n the first of October 1874 the carriageway of Dublin's newest bridge was opened to traffic. Crossing from Capel Street on the city's north side to Parliament Street on the south, the as yet unnamed bridge was not quite finished – the pedestrian walkways were incomplete, the ironworks unpainted and the decorative lamp standards unchosen. In January 1875 the bridge was named for Henry Grattan, reformist and parliamentarian, and by May it was finally completed.

Construction had began in June 1873. The contract was not for a totally new bridge but for the lowering and widening of the old bridge, thus today's structure – designed by eminent Dublin Port and Docks engineer, the splendidly named Bindon Blood Stoney – is much in the style of that it replaced: a masonry bridge of five arches but with a lower gradient to better accommodate traffic. By necessity the shape and size of the outer arches were altered – Dublin Corporation was planning a new mains drainage scheme and two low-level, red-brick sewers were built into the abutments. Thus, whilst the centre arches are elliptical in shape (to achieve a low rise), the smaller, side arches are semi-circular. In addition these side arches were constructed first and the three central arches constructed in tandem to neutralise the horizontal thrust on the piers.

In substance too Grattan Bridge owes much to its predecessor – the foundation, piers and arches are largely those built in the mid-18th century by the innovative engineer, George Semple, who declared his foundations were constructed 'to last as long as the Sugar Loaf'. In an exercise of 19th-century recycling much of the hewn stone was re-dressed and used again in the arch sheeting while the face voussoirs, ashlars and wing walls were dressed in new granite.

Widening of the bridge was accomplished by cantilevering footpaths out from the east and west faces. These, along with the parapets, are supported

The first bridge here was opened in 1676 to a design by Humphrey Jervis. In 1722 an equestrian statue of George I (below) was erected on a pedestal upstream of the bridge. The statue was removed during the reconstruction of the 1750s.

122

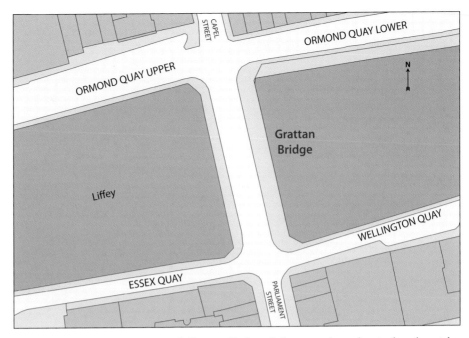

Overleaf: a busy scene, looking upriver, in front of the (then) Custom House with the 'new' Essex Bridge, of 1755, built by George Semple. A pioneer in the use of cofferdams, he declared his foundations were constructed 'to last as long as the Sugar Loaf'.

by cast-iron consoles, beautifully scrolled and decorated in classical style with pateras and rosettes, as well as ornamental acanthus leaves. These consoles rest on small granite shelves or corbels which project from each upper pier. Each distinctive, lattice-work iron parapet is laid out in five sections interspaced by six cast-iron dadoes topped with nail head panels. On each of these rests a cast-iron lamp standard, characterised by elegant, outwardly facing seahorses. The standards added £240 to the overall cost of the bridge.

There is a long history of bridge building here in the heart of the old city. In 1676 Humphrey Jervis, politician and developer, built the first crossing on this site: Essex Bridge connected newly laid-out Capel Street, lined with fashionable Dutch-style mansions to what were then the rambling medieval streets and lanes on the south side. Parliament Street was not laid out until 1758 when the new science of urban planning stipulated that the streets approaching a bridge must be the same width as the bridge itself.

Jervis' construction was Dublin's third bridge and its most easterly at that time. It was a seven-arch masonry bridge – it is told that Jervis had his workers commandeer many of the stones required from the nearby St Mary's Abbey which dates from the 12th century. The bridge foundations consisted of simple timber grilles, most likely constructed off site and lowered onto the river bed. A timber drawbridge, later removed, allowed ships to pass upstream. This old Essex Bridge was a living bridge, lined with shops and houses, dense with people, driving their carts or herding their livestock to and from the city. Sailing ships from far and wide unloaded their exotic cargoes nearby at the old Custom House where merchandise was assessed for payment of the kings' taxes.

Old Essex Bridge, built as it was directly onto the river bed, underwent many repairs and rebuilds in its history. In 1687 raging Liffey flood waters

I.Tudor delin.

Publish'd according to

A Prospect of the Custom House, and Essex Bridge, DUBLIN.

London, Printed, for Robt. Sayer Map & Printseller

rliament.
Veüe de la Doüane, et Dupont d'Essex, a DUBLIN.
Golden Back near Serjeants Inn, Fleet Street.

Parr Sculp.

VIEW FROM *CAPEL-STREET, LOOKING OVER ESSEX-BRIDGE__DUBLIN.*

London Published Oct. 1797. by Jas. Malton.

caused a major collapse of the north-side arch, sweeping a hackney coach, its driver and horses into the river.

In 1722 a commanding statue of George I, gazing regally towards the sea and his dominions beyond, was erected on a large pier which abutted from the western side of the bridge. Then in 1751, George Semple, who started as a bricklayer, and practised as an architect, engineer and builder, designed temporary repairs, using timber, for fallen piers and arches, and the bridge was reopened to traffic.

In 1752 the bridge was deemed irreparable. Construction of a new Essex Bridge began on the 19th January 1753, funded by a citizens' lottery. Semple, chosen as designer and contractor, was an innovative man. He made the first ever use of cofferdams – watertight structures built below water level and pumped dry for the construction of foundations – in Irish bridge construction. The rubble on the river bed from the old bridge, as well as the plinth for the George I statue, were removed, as the diversion of water was judged to have caused damage to the old bridge. The five span, semi-circular stone arch bridge was completed in April 1755 at a cost of over £20,000. Economies were made by reusing the stone taken from the abbey though, extravagantly

Above: Malton's print of 1797, looking from Capel Street, south along Essex Bridge, with the Royal Exchange (now City Hall) at the end of the vista.

George Semple pioneered the use of cofferdams in his construction of Essex Bridge in 1755. Water was pumped out from within these and work could proceed to secure good foundations, well founded under the river bed. Right: a plate from his book 'A Treatise on Building in Water' shows a section of 'the Pump Engine'.

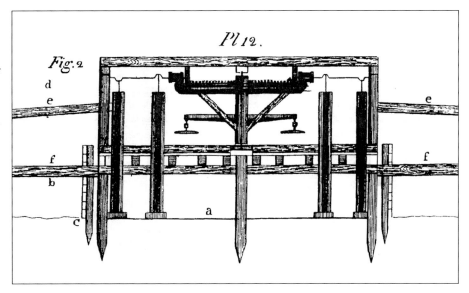

George Semple pioneered the use of cofferdams in his construction of Essex Bridge in 1755. Water was pumped out from within these and work could proceed to secure good foundations, well founded under the river bed. Right: a plate from his book 'A Treatise on Building in Water' shows a section of 'the Pump Engine'.

for the time, 20 globe-style oil lamps were placed which illuminated the bridge at night. The new Essex Bridge was modelled on London's Westminster Bridge though its designer boasted that it was wider. It would serve Dublin until remodelled and rebuilt to become the Grattan Bridge of 1875.

Naming Dublin's bridges and streets for those who held power was, through the centuries of British dominance over Ireland, an established custom. Thus Jervis chose to name his bridge of 1676 for Arthur Capell (1631-1683), Lord Essex and Irish Viceroy in 1672. Capell, an honest man, set about disclosing the rampant corruption of the Dublin administration, describing Ireland as a country where 'everyone pulls and tears what he can for himself'. As he worked against using Irish taxes for the rebuilding of Windsor Castle and the financing of the king's mistress, his enemies lobbied energetically to have him recalled, which he duly was in 1677. Semple's groundbreaking new structure of 1755 adopted the old name, though to this day the bridge is often called simply 'Capel Street Bridge'.

By the time of naming the new bridge of 1875, a new set of political circumstances applied. Catholics now had the right to vote, could now work in the professions and had gained control of many municipal corporations, including Dublin's. Grattan Bridge was named for Henry Grattan, a wealthy and privileged lawyer who turned to politics and fought for greater independence for Ireland. His greatest victories came in the years of 'Grattan's Parliament' when even from the opposition benches his powerful oratory and political acumen wrung free trade and some legislative independence – short-lived as the Act of Union came into force in 1801. Grattan had a love of walking by the Liffey deep in thought, honing his political philosophy.

At the rise of the bridge on the east and west sides there are identical bronze commemorative plaques: 'Essex Bridge erected 1755; rebuilt by the Dublin Port & Docks Board 1875; renamed Grattan Bridge by the Municipal Council 1875; the Right Hon. BLE Peter Paul McSwiney; J.P. High Sheriff; Bindon B. Stoney Engineer; V.J. Doherty. Contractor.'

Below: statue of Henry Grattan (1746-1820) at College Green. In 1875, the bridge was renamed after this skilled orator and politician who campaigned for Irish Parliamentary freedom.

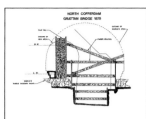

Above: during the 1875 construction, cofferdams were also necessary.

Left: decorative cast-iron sea horses grace the lamp standards. These were cast by the Dublin ironmasters, Mallets, for the bridge reconstruction of 1875.

Below: President John F. Kennedy seen crossing the bridge, during his visit to Ireland in 1963.

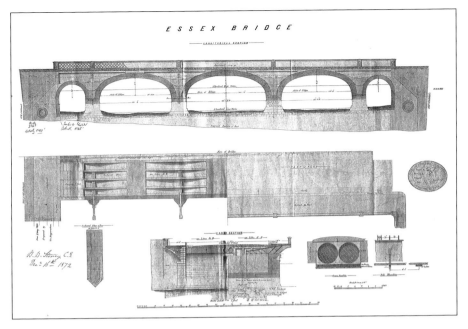

In the second half of the 19th century it was decided to carry out a major reconstruction of the bridge, to increase the width and flatten the gradients across it. Right: newly flat and wide – details of the 1875 structure.

The Structure

Grattan Bridge is a five-arch masonry structure with a total span of 52 metres. It carries road and pedestrian traffic.

The foundations are of rough masonry laid between timber sheet piles and along with the abutments and piers are largely those of the previous structure dating to 1755. Cofferdams, composing two layers of parallel 150 mm dovetailed oak piles into which blue clay was placed, were used in the construction of the arches and piers. The timber was driven to rock and cut off at the surface on completion.

The three central arches are of flat elliptical shape while, springing from the abutments adjacent to the north and south quays, the two smaller arches are semi-circular. Their reduced size and different shaping was necessary to provide space for the construction of the main drainage sewers. All four piers have cutwaters on both the east and west faces. The masonry is evenly coursed granite ashlar throughout, being rusticated on the archrings and upper portions of the piers. On both east and west sides the footpaths are cantilevered 2.4 metres from the bridge face and are carried, along with the parapet, on a total of eight large, cast iron-consoles. Each in turn rests on a small granite corbel projecting from the chamfered upper portion of each pier. Each parapet, of riveted iron lattice work, is in five sections alternating with six cast-iron dadoes with nail head panels each crowned with a cast-iron lamp. The lamp standards are adorned with rampant seahorses.

The cost of Grattan Bridge is recorded as £25,380 7s 6d. The bridge date of 1875, the engineer Bindon Blood Stoney along with other details are presented on bronze commemorative plaques on both the east and west sides.

The bridge decks and pathways, found to be suffering from an ingress of water, were upgraded in 2002 at a cost of €2.3 million. Uniquely, the upgrade included the fixing of the adjacent Liffey boardwalk to the bridge.

Below: the bridge is decorated by eight cast-iron consoles which act as cantilevers supporting the side footpaths.

MILLENNIUM BRIDGE

DROICHEAD NA MÍLAOISE

CROSSES FROM ORMOND QUAY LOWER TO WELLINGTON QUAY

PEDESTRIAN BRIDGE   METAL   1999

In the thousand years of the history of Dublin's bridges, the Millennium Bridge was only the second footbridge built to cross the Liffey. A steel and concrete structure, the bridge is a thoroughly modern take on its historic neighbour 125 metres downstream, the Ha'penny Bridge, Dublin's original pedestrian bridge.

Construction of the Millennium, the city's first new bridge since the East-Link of 1984, was problematic – the centre city location was always busy, the narrow quays bordering the site had severe traffic congestion and the contract time was a mere six months. The solution was to utilise the river itself as a construction base and to assemble the bridge superstructure off site. To this end a large pontoon was moored in the river, working platforms were constructed from there and work progressed on a 24 hour cycle as the tides permitted.

The 60-tonne structure, fully completed with balustrades and integrated lighting, was prefabricated off site by Thompson Engineering, Carlow and in an operation lasting an half hour, on Sunday 7th November 1999, was lifted off its road transporter, swung out over the river and onto the already prepared concrete bridge supports. A mere six weeks later, on Monday 20th December, the bridge was opened to the public – 11 days ahead of schedule.

Safeguarding the visual character and qualities of the area – a designated conservation area – was integral to the project. The new bridge had to radiate lightness and transparency: the gaze of the bridge user drawn to the river and its surrounding architecture. Steel was the ideal material and the very slender nature of the structural members used produced the lightness and elegance required.

An Irish product in design and manufacture, the Millennium Bridge is a truss bridge. The truss itself in an asymmetrical parabolic arch – a gentle, inverted-U shape – complementing its venerable neighbour, the Ha'penny Bridge.

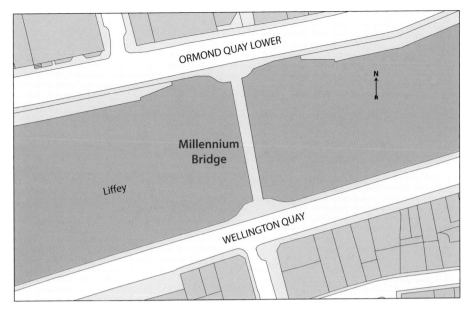

The curving abutment walls, gradually open the river view to the approaching bridge user by stepping down the characteristic granite blocks of the quay walls. The bridge railings are also of steel, topped with a simple aluminium bronze handrail – an irresistible invitation to lean and enjoy the river. In a gentle, wave-like motion the railings swell slightly outwards at mid-point.

The width of the Liffey here is 51 metres, though the bridge span accounts for only 41 metres of that as the abutments jut out into the river carrying the tapering pavement to meet the bridge itself. This point is marked, north and south, by tall lamp standards reminiscent of a sentinel at the old city gates. The concrete bridge haunches are contained within these abutments which are themselves clad with Wicklow granite in keeping with the appearance of other Liffey bridges. As the tide ebbs and flows the abutments are gradually concealed and revealed – bridge and river working in harmony.

Lighting is a special feature of the Millennium Bridge. Children delight in skipping from one to another of the runway-style uplighters centred along the deck. And as dusk deepens and darkness falls the glass globe lighting atop the lamp standards turn from white to midnight blue. The handrails are lit by hidden emitters and the latticework of the understructure is illuminated by narrow-beam floodlights tucked under the pavement of the abutments.

The bridge deck is of silver aluminium plank and there is a gentle gradient which, along with the absence of steps at the thresholds, makes the bridge user friendly for all.

Dublin Corporation's inspired Millennium Project sought submissions for a bridge design for the site in 1998 – the prize fund was £10,000. It was not the first time a bridge had been proposed for the area but in the 1980s the unfavourable economic climate put paid to any such project and the south river bank very nearly became home to a large central bus station. In the early 1990s a proposal for what was termed a 'wibbly wobbly bridge', link-

Left: the simple steelwork of the assymetric parabolic arch.

ing Meeting House Square in the newly-emerging Temple Bar cultural area and the north quays caught the public imagination, but not the city planners' agreement. As the clock ticked towards the year 2000 and the economic tide turned the planners had reason, resources and enthusiasm for a new look at the area.

Thus, the Millennium Bridge became a focus of civic pride for the city and one from which up to five million people a year would benefit. The competition was run in association with the Institution of Engineers of Ireland and received 153 entries from across the world. From a shortlist of six, Howley Harrington Architects with Price and Myers as Consultant Engineers, were selected.

The quality of design and construction is such that on opening it received an array of awards from such as the Institution of Structural Engineers, the Royal Institute of the Architects of Ireland, the Royal Institute of British Architects, the Construction Industry Federation, the Architectural Review Emerging Architecture award and Opus Plan Expo 2000.

With a little bit of Dublin wit and in keeping with a tradition of decorative manhole covers across the city, stainless steel commemorative plaques are embedded in the north and south manholes of the bridge. In ever-decreasing circles, such as a stone might form when dropped into water, the details of the bridge are recorded: John Fitzgerald, City Manager; Michael Phillips, City Engineer; Tim Brick, Deputy City Engineer; designed by Howley Harrington Architects; Price and Myers, Engineers; constructed by Ascon Ltd; officially opened for the year 2000, by the Rt. Hon. Lord Mayor, Cllr. Mary Freehill, The Millennium Bridge, Dublin Corporation.

Below: like a stone dropped into water – stainless steel plaque, also doubling as a manhole, commemorating the opening of the bridge in December 1999.

*Right: high tension –
heavy lift. Craning the
new bridge into place.*

The Structure

The Millennium Bridge is a steel truss structure crossing the Liffey in a single span of 41 metres from Ormond Quay Lower on the north bank to Wellington Quay on the south. The truss is designed as an asymmetrical parabolic arch, the booms of which are made of single steel rod and curve gently inward in plan and section from the abutments on the north and south river banks.

A simple and highly efficient pin-footed portal frame, the bridge structure terminates in the large concrete haunches contained within the shell abutments. These curving abutment walls, clad in granite, act as spread-waters.

A pedestrian-only bridge, the deck of slotted aluminium planks rises gently – the gradient is 1 in 20 – and then flattens in mid section. This is supported off a series of secondary ribs running between the cross members. These are integral with the top booms of the truss and continue upwards to provide supports for the balustrade and leaning rail.

The deck is lit using hidden emitters supplied by fibre optic harnesses running inside the specially shaped aluminium bronze handrails. A series of uplighters, similar to runway lights, also guide the bridge user at night. Two lamp standards, topped with small glass globes, illuminate each bridge end. The abutment parapets reflect the detail of the existing quay walls by stepping down the granite stonework in semi-circular sweeps as the pavement curves out over the river, thus opening up the bridge width at each end.

The bridge was designed by Howley Harrington Architects and the cost was £1.6 million. On both the north and south thresholds of the bridge a stainless steel commemorative plaque, also serving as a manhole cover, records the opening of the Millennium Bridge on 20th December 1999.

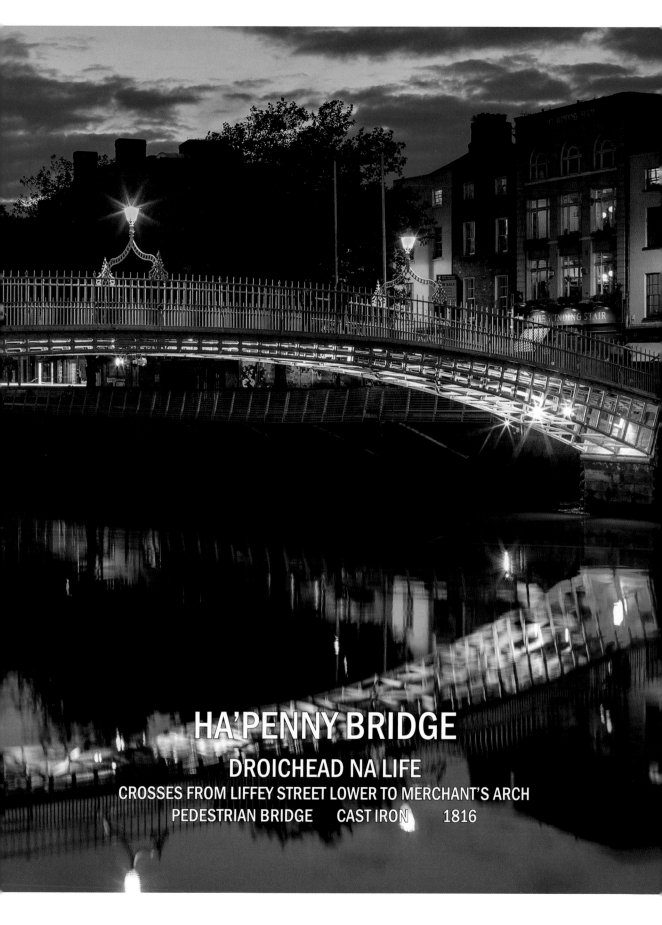

HA'PENNY BRIDGE

DROICHEAD NA LIFE

CROSSES FROM LIFFEY STREET LOWER TO MERCHANT'S ARCH

PEDESTRIAN BRIDGE   CAST IRON   1816

The Ha'penny Bridge is the first pedestrian-only crossing of the Liffey and the sixth oldest in the family of Liffey bridges. It connects the junction of Ormond Quay Lower and Liffey Street Lower on the north bank to Merchant's Arch on Wellington Quay to the south.

The distinctive single elliptical arch structure has come to symbolise the quirky, friendly, jaunty nature of Dublin city to visitors and citizens alike. And like the city itself, the Ha'penny Bridge is a unique and elegant mixture of the old and the new.

The essential fabric of the bridge is that cast 200 years ago at the Coalbrookdale Iron Foundry in Shropshire, England. Abraham Darby III's ironworks was at the cutting edge of the Industrial Revolution. The works had produced the world's first cast-iron bridge (the aptly named Iron Bridge, over the River Severn, in 1781). In the early years of railway construction it made cast-iron rails. It provided a series of Doric cast-iron columns for the new Dublin and Drogheda Railway in 1844, that carry the railway at high level over Sheriff Street in Dublin.

The cast-iron members that would make up the Ha'penny Bridge were transported to Dublin on sailing ships and erected on site. Granite abutments had already been prepared and the three arch ribs – each in six sections – were arranged in a parallel formation with cross and diagonal bracing and onto which a timber gangway was built. As with many crossings of the time the bridge was to be tolled. 'Receiving houses', or toll booths, were constructed at each threshold. Lighting was provided by lanterns atop the delightful twin S-shaped or transverse ogee arches.

Once a ferry plied its trade here, operated by a city alderman, William Walsh, who was also granted the 99-year lease for the operation of the toll of the new pedestrian bridge. It offered a lucrative business opportunity: passengers were now guaranteed a safer – and dryer – short cut to locations on the southside like the popular Crow Street Theatre. Magnanimously Walsh granted the citizens of Dublin 10 toll-free days on his new bridge when it

The ironfoundry at Coalbrookdale was literally at the crucible of the Industrial Revolution. It produced the world's first cast-iron bridge in 1781. The 1816 Ha'penny Bridge was cast at Coalbrookdale and shipped to Dublin. The Doric columns for the railway bridge at Sheriff Street (below) also came from Coalbrookdale, for the Dublin & Drogheda Railway in 1844.

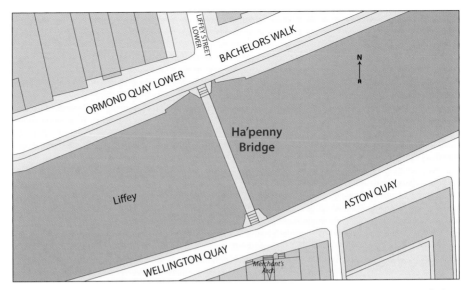

*Below: the world's first
arch bridge made of cast
iron, (cast at nearby
Coalbrookdale) over the
River Severn, at Iron-
bridge Gorge, Shropshire,
England.*

first opened in 1816 – a timely gesture given that he had been told that if the bridge was found objectionable by the people he would have to take it down again. But with an average 450 pedestrian crossings a day, Walsh came to enjoy an annual income of around £330 from the venture. He was also granted £3,000 compensation for the loss of his ferry business – that amount being also the reported cost of the bridge.

On opening, the bridge was named for Arthur Wellesley (1769-1852), Duke of Wellington, hero of the Battle of Waterloo. The third of six children, Arthur was a disappointment to his family who could never quite remember in which month he had been born or whether he had made his first appearance in Dublin or at the family seat, Castle Dangan in Co. Meath. He was thought to be of idle and indifferent character and was dispatched to the army. As it turned out, this unpromising youth was to enjoy a stellar military and political career, serving two terms as Prime Minister of the United Kingdom. Noted as a conservative and 'reluctant Irishman' he nevertheless supported Catholic emancipation.

Despite his popularity following the defeat of Napoleon, the name Wellington Bridge never quite caught the public imagination. Dubliners preferred the name 'Ha'penny Bridge' or even the 'Iron', 'Metal' or 'Triangle Bridge'. The ordnance survey map of 1834 labels it the 'Liffey Bridge'.

Over the course of its two centuries, not everybody professed a love of the bridge. The Irish art collector Hugh Lane (who was considering handing over his unique collection of French art to the Dublin Municipal Gallery) described it as an "ugly metal footbridge" and offered the city a "most beautiful and remarkable" alternative. Lane's proposal, drawn up by the celebrated architect, Edwin Lutyens, was for an elliptical-arch stone bridge connecting elaborate pavilions on either side of the river, each housing modern art (including Lane's collection). Another gallery on the bridge would house a smaller collection. Yeats wrote of it, "I have seen the Lutyens design – beauti-

Above: an idealised view of the Regency city. The citizenry stroll and enjoy the Liffeyside, as the new footbridge elegantly spans the river.

ful". This wonderful adornment of the river, it was said, would call to mind Florence's Uffizi Gallery and the Ponte Vecchio.

On 28th March 1913 Dublin Corporation formally adopted Lane's plan for the replacement of the Ha'penny Bridge. Later, divisions emerged – an Irish architect was demanded, the riverside location was seen as unsuitable for a gallery while others argued that the money could be better spent on housing for Dublin's poor. The bridge-gallery was not built. Lane dispatched his collection to London (though it is now, in part, shared between Dublin and London) and the Ha'penny Bridge was saved.

In 1919 pedestrians no longer had to pay to cross the bridge and the turnstiles were removed. In 1923 it was officially renamed the Liffey Bridge.

In the course of the 20th century the Ha'penny Bridge was at various times painted in shades of green, silver and even black. For a time around the mid century, unsightly advertising boards such as that for Spratt's Patent Dog Cakes, adorned the bridge. The wooden deck was at some time covered with asphalt, the bridge walkways flattened at either end, missing rails were not replaced and unsightly scaffolding propped it up in places. At one stage it was bathed in an improbable blue light.

Dublin Corporation commissioned a timely assessment of the bridge in 1998. Conserving the Ha'penny Bridge as purely ornamental was considered but it was decided that it served best as a working bridge and a refurbishment was ordered. The project brought together engineers and conser-

Right: beautiful? W. B. Yeats thought so. Schematic of Edwin Lutyens' proposal for a Gallery of Modern Art, located on a new bridge over the river, replacing the Ha'penny Bridge.

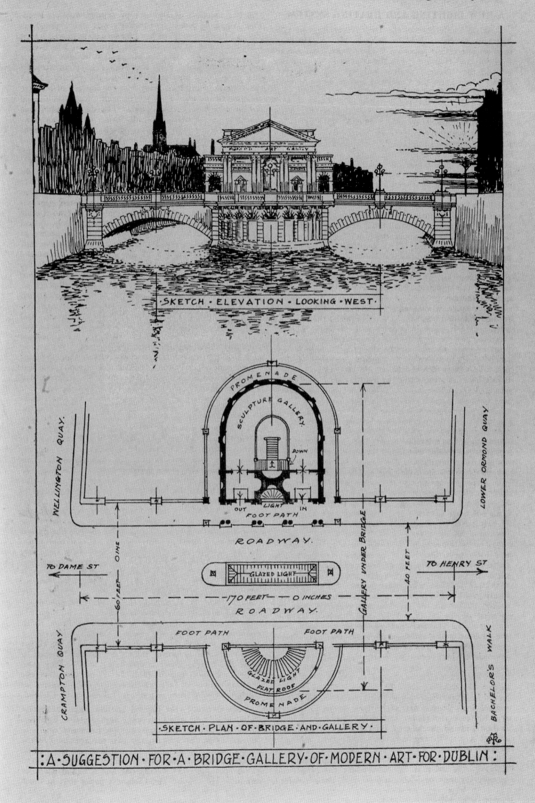

· SKETCH · ELEVATION · LOOKING · WEST ·

· SKETCH · PLAN · OF · BRIDGE · AND · GALLERY ·

: · A · SUGGESTION · FOR · A · BRIDGE · GALLERY · OF · MODERN · ART · FOR · DUBLIN · :

Left: Dubliners have always had an affinity with the Ha'penny Bridge. A scene from 1949.

vationists who considered a total of 52 different design options. In due course a temporary Bailey bridge was erected and the Ha'penny Bridge was closed in early 2001.

On examination, the superstructure proved sound. The focus now was on the corroded railings and deck. Over 1,000 individual rail pieces were labelled, carefully removed and sent for repair and restoration. The vertical alignment of the deck was restored to its original profile and a new deck floor of stiffened steel was installed, covered with a slip resistant epoxy finish. Safer entrance and exit points were created for pedestrians by widening, curving and smoothening the bridge mouths.

Subtle recessed lighting replaced the garish 1980s-style lamps and finally the bridge was repainted in the original off-white colour. Retaining as much of the original fabric of the bridge was paramount and 98% of the original ironwork was re-used. Those bars which were replicated were done in such a way as to have the slightly worn and pitted surface characteristic of the old bridge railings. Such was the quality of the work that in 2003 it was recognised by a European Union Cultural Heritage/Europa Nostra Award, Europe's most prestigious heritage prize. The Ha'penny Bridge re-opened on 21st December 2001.

Below: conservation work underway. Over 1,000 individual rail pieces were labelled, carefully removed and sent for repair and restoration. The bridge was repainted in the original off-white colour. Completely refurbished, it reopened in December 2001.

Right: an icon of Dublin. The Ha'penny Bridge is one of the most-photographed sights of the city.

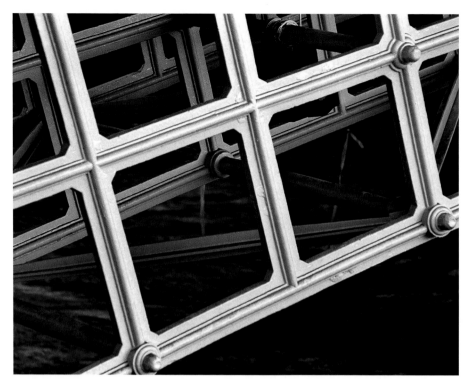

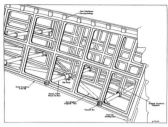

Above: the design, and left, the reality. Cast-iron ribs.

The Structure

The Ha'penny Bridge is a single elliptical-arch structure with a span of 42.8 metres. The bridge width is 3.6 metres and it rises 3.35 metres at the crown above high water, giving a low rise-to-span ratio. A pedestrian-only bridge, it was cast at the Coalbrookdale, Shropshire works of Abraham Darby III under the guidance of John Windsor.

The cast-iron superstructure is composed of three parallel arch ribs – one on each side and one in the centre. Each of these is in six segments which are connected at each joint by six bolts through a single continuous plate. The ribs are cruciform sections offering greater resistance than a flat plate. Compression forces are taken by deflection of the arch, while tension forces are taken by the six bolts at the rib joints. The granite abutments each extend over 4.3 metres from the quays into the river.

Extensive refurbishment took place in 2001. The cast-iron arches and railings were disassembled for repair and restoration off site with due care and attention given to retaining as large a portion of the old iron as possible.

Lighting installed in the 1980s was replaced with more subtle recessed lighting and the bridge mouths were widened for the comfort and safety of users. Further lighting is provided by three lanterns on transverse ogee arches.

The vertical alignment of the deck was restored to its original profile and ease of access further improved by the addition of stepped ramps on either threshold. A new deck of stiffened steel, with a slip resistant epoxy finish, was provided. The project, which was completed in a year, cost £1.25 million.

A commemorative plaque records the original date of the bridge – 1816 – and its reopening on 21st December 2001.

Chapter 3

O'CONNELL BRIDGE TO THE SEA
Ó DHROICHEAD UÍ CHONAILL GO DTÍ AN FHARRAIGE

Anna Livia keystone from the former Carlisle Bridge

The bridges at the eastern end of the Liffey date from the end of the 19th century to the present and are of concrete and steel construction. The designs range from the spectacular yet elegant Calatrava-designed Samuel Beckett Bridge to prosaic Butt Bridge and include O'Connell Bridge, the most important and widest of Dublin's bridges that connects the principal thoroughfare with the south city. Not all that we encounter here are road bridges: there is a modern footbridge, a bridge to carry the Luas and the heavily-engineered Loop Line Bridge, which carries the busy DART service.

O'CONNELL BRIDGE

DROICHEAD UÍ CHONAILL
CROSSES FROM O'CONNELL STREET TO WESTMORELAND STREET
ROAD AND LIGHT RAIL BRIDGE   MASONRY ARCH   1880

On 6th August 1880 the Right Honourable Edmund Dwyer Gray, newspaper proprietor and Lord Mayor of Dublin, declared the city's newest bridge fully open. The bemused populace, gathered on the bridge, gave a loud cheer when he announced that it was to be known as O'Connell Bridge.

O'Connell Bridge was built to replace the Carlisle Bridge of 1794. That bridge, designed by James Gandon, was by the mid-19th century, in poor condition and lying unevenly on its foundations – and described as 'the most dangerous bridge in the empire'. It required policemen with batons to clear the bottlenecks and traffic congestion. Clearly a new bridge was needed. From as early as 1841 the public were treated to designs for its replacement: the Royal Academy Exhibition of that year featured a model which demonstrated the widening of the old structure. Just over 20 years later Dublin Corporation announced a bridge design competition and from 60 entries the winner was chosen – a single span cast-iron arched bridge. In the event, for whatever reason, the winning design, by George Page and Ballsbridge ironfounder Richard Turner (who had made the great palm houses at Kew Gardens, as well as at the Botanic Gardens in Glasnevin), was never built.

In 1868 the recently established Port and Docks Board was approved by Parliament to take up the matter and it instructed its engineer, Bindon Blood Stoney to proceed. Four tenders were submitted and that of William J. Doherty was approved. Doherty, who had worked on Grattan Bridge, included the construction of yet another bridge, the swivel Butt Bridge, in his tender.

In July 1877 Doherty moved on site. Construction was contracted to take two and a half years with a £30 per week penalty for time overrun. Stoney's clever design allowed for a portion of the bridge to be in use at all times

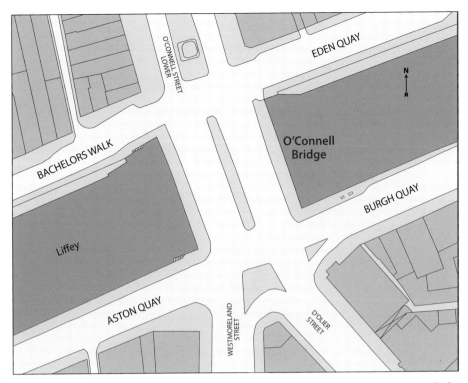

throughout construction. The first sections of the new bridge were appended onto the old structure, part of which remained open. By 10th June 1879, a new side addition was open to the public though as yet no parapet had been built – Doherty was keen to get on with demolishing the old piers and building the new central section.

As the work progressed, Dubliners by the Liffey witnessed almost surreal sights as slowly, through the mists and rains of autumn and early winter, the old arches were demolished and the new section was built upon the remains of the old piers. Stoney's eminently classical design mimicked the bridge of old yet improved upon that narrow, humpbacked structure by being almost three times as wide and having a lower gradient. While retaining Gandon's three arches, Stoney replaced the semi circular with the elliptical and as the old keystones would no longer fit, new representations of Anna Livia and the Atlantic were sculpted by Charles V. Harrison.

A simple sandstone parapet was provided. It had balusters interspaced with dadoes decorated with elegant, three-arm, Parisian lamp standards. The central island was lit by three, five-arm standards. In contrast to the well-cut granite ashlar of the arches and lower piers, the upper piers are rusticated or roughened and decorated with pleasant garlands. Stoney thoughtfully located doorways to the gas and water pipes under the central arches and out of view.

The final bill was £70,342 4s 1d – no penalty was incurred despite a six month time overrun as the bridge had never actually closed to traffic. Difficulties when solid rock was encountered, severe weather and the gas mains not being ready, contributed to the delays.

Engraved by T.Barber, from a Drawing by Geo Petrie, for the Picture of Dublin

SACKVILLE STREET, POST OFFICE & NELSON'S COLUMN.

Published by Willm Curry Junr & Co Dublin August 1839.

By May 1880 all that remained was to name the bridge. Controversy arose when both the Port and Docks Board, who had commissioned the bridge and Dublin Corporation claimed the right to name it. Prior to opening, the Board had installed a plaque of Aberdeen marble. It read: 'Carlisle Bridge; Built 1794; Rebuilt 1880'. Enraged members of the Corporation threatened to retaliate by painting the name 'O'Connell' on every stone and lamp post of the bridge. A compromise to the well-publicised dispute was eventually reached and a brass plaque commemorating the opening of O'Connell Bridge, previously Carlisle Bridge, now discreetly covers the offending piece of marble.

Controversy too had dogged Carlisle Bridge, the first on this site. In the late 18th century, rival business and political interests clashed over the location of the proposed new bridge. At stake was the dominance of Dublin's old medieval quarter, well served by bridges, and the rise of the eastern city around the newly-fashionable Sackville Street, which by 1790 stretched all the way to the river. But by the time architect James Gandon arrived in Dublin, to begin the design of the new Custom House, the city's eastward shift had became unstoppable. Gandon got the commission to build the new bridge – his initial grand design, with a triumphal arch, colonnaded walkways and an equestrian statue of the king was rejected in favour of a cheaper, three-arch

Above: a graceful scene. 'Sackville Street, Post Office & Nelson's Column', in this early Victorian view from Carlisle Bridge.

152

Above: smaller river boats were able to travel upstream under Carlisle Bridge, then the most easterly of the bridges over the Liffey.

Right: a pre-1880 photograph of Carlisle Bridge. The rise in the 18th-century bridge can be clearly seen, in contrast to its replacement by O'Connell Bridge, which is flatter.

Above: work underway on Stoney's replacement bridge. Sailing ships are still able to moor close by.

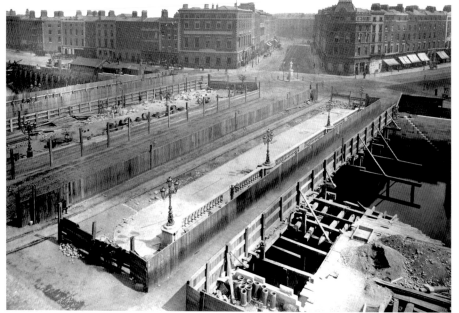

Left: the 1880 bridge is in the last stage of construction. The first set of the elegant lamp standards, manufactured in Paris, has been erected. Note the temporary footbridge to the right.

Above: the 'Atlantic' head (carved by eminent sculptor Edward Smyth), originally located on Gandon's Carlisle Bridge. It was removed during the 1880 reconstruction as it would not fit on the new bridge. It is now on the facade of the former Tropical Fruit Warehouse on Sir John Rogerson's Quay.

Below: the replacement 'Atlantic' carved head on the keystone of O'Connell Bridge.

bridge of Portland stone and granite, with a simple but elegant parapet. It included keystones: Anna Livia and the Atlantic, sculpted by Edward Smyth whose statues adorn the Four Courts and the Custom House. During the construction of Stoney's later bridge, these did not fit in the new arch and were relocated to the facade of the (then) Tropical Fruit Company warehouse on Sir John Rogerson's Quay. The parapet, removed by Doherty, was placed at his mansion in Drumcondra, Clonturk House.

Gandon's bridge was named for Frederick Howard, the 5th Earl of Carlisle, English diplomat and Lord Lieutenant (Viceroy) of Ireland between 1780 and 1782. A poet and playwright – he was related to Lord Byron – Carlisle was considered an able administrator and an excellent society host. His support for the new bridge was crucial to the necessary finance being granted by parliament.

Naming the new bridge of 1880 for Daniel O'Connell was a bolder move, designed to break the tradition of naming Dublin's bridges and streets in honour of English viceroys. O'Connell, a peerless political activist, lawyer, family man and bon viveur was born in Kerry in 1775. Educated in France, from whence he fled during the violent turmoil of the revolution, he studied law in London. He enjoyed life at the expense of a rich uncle and formed his radical political ideas. A handsome man and a fine orator, he grew a mass political movement, characterised by peaceful, yet persuasive resistance and brilliant organisation. He could command a crowd of many thousands and enthuse them for Ireland and its freedom without a drop of blood being spilled. His aims were full and equal rights for Irish Catholics, an underclass in their own country – which was achieved in 1829 – and self governance for Ireland, of which he was even more convinced, having witnessed the horrors of the mid-century Great Famine and the lackadaisical and desultory reaction of the London government. O'Connell worked tirelessly for other causes too – prison reform and the abolishment of slavery – and, in 1841, was elected the first Catholic Lord Mayor of Dublin since 1690. He died in Genoa in 1847.

O'Connell Bridge has stood witness to many of the great moments in Irish history. The leaders of 1916 passed in sight of here en route to the GPO on Easter Monday 1916. Later that week, as the sun burned down from a clear blue sky, O'Connell Bridge, normally swarming with traffic, was a virtual no-man's land in the centre of a war zone, except for the lone figure of a man lying outstretched, felled by a sniper. Beyond him, flames licked the sky from many buildings on Dublin's grand boulevard, Sackville Street. The buildings which abutted the bridge on the northern quays were also ablaze. Everywhere there was noise of battle – from the rifles, machine guns and later artillery of the British, on the roofs and streets south of the Liffey. These exchanged fire across the bridge with the Volunteers in their outposts around Sackville Street. When the Rising was over, mere days later, prisoners were marched down the quays, passing by the bridge, as bystanders stared.

O'Connell Bridge was a favourite picket point for the British during the War of Independence from 1919 to 1921. By day soldiers stood watch and by

night revolving searchlights beamed out across the bridge. As that war drew to a close, the burning of the Custom House drew crowds onto the bridge. The truce of July 1921 was celebrated with ships downstream sounding their steam sirens and barges blowing their whistles as they passed under the bridge.

Dubliners crowded against the parapets to witness the opening scenes of the Irish Civil War in June 1922. To the west was the great dome of the Four Courts, shrouded in early morning mist, the building occupied by men, once comrades in arms with the forces of the new Provisional Government but now bitter enemies. On Friday, 30th June a great explosion rocked the city. A dark cloud mushroomed above the Four Courts and one thousand years of public records flew skywards and then to rest on the city streets – and on O'Connell Bridge. Ignoring the danger of stray bullets and displaying the same curiosity as in 1916, onlookers assembled at the south end of O'Connell Bridge to observe the conflict which had spread to Sackville Street. Another chapter in the Civil War occurred when, in August 1922, in a procession lasting one hour and 35 minutes, the funeral of Michael Collins passed this way.

Above: an 1890s scene looking downriver from O'Connell Bridge. With Butt Bridge and its central swivel span in the background, the Custom House, in the distance, is obscured by the newly-constructed Loop Line Bridge. A horse-drawn tram is beginning its journey to the affluent suburb of Rathmines.

Above: a 1950s post-card. Buses and cars cross O'Connell Bridge, as a Guinness barge sails upriver.

Below: many decades ago, city traffic was lighter than it is today. Reflecting those less-complicated times, a Garda Síochána controls traffic over O'Connell Bridge.

In more peaceful times, on 26th June 1932 Cardinal Lorenzo Lauri made the closing address of the Eucharistic Congress from O'Connell Bridge to an estimated gathering of one million people.

From time to time the architecture of O'Connell Bridge has been altered – the parapet lamps were peremptorily reduced to one arm in 1919 but the classical three-arm design was restored in the 1990s. A large copper bowl, filled with plastic 'flames' immersed in water, decorated the bridge briefly in 1953 but met its fate, courtesy of a young student, at the bottom of the Liffey.

Restoration work has been carried out over the years. The parapet lamps were further refurbished and repaired in 2002. Increasingly high tides caused water damage and erosion to the pillars and balustrades and these were repaired by Dublin City Council in 2008.

All told, O'Connell Bridge seems hardly a mere structure – more a destination at the very heart of Dublin.

157

Above: the bridge and river as a venue for leisure in 1923 – 'The Liffey Swim', by Jack B. Yeats. It depicts the swim as it approaches O'Connell Bridge.

Left: the bridge was part of the backdrop to the conflict in central Dublin during 1916. This is a photograph from the immediate aftermath of Easter Week. British soldiers escort a prisoner over O'Connell Bridge. In the background, Hopkins and Hopkins, Jewellers, and other buildings along Eden Quay, can be seen in ruins.

*Above: the bridge and
quayside as a venue for
commerce in 1889 – 'A
Vendor of Books' by Walter
Frederick Osborne. It
shows a busy book stall
on Aston Quay with the
newly-rebuilt O'Connell
Bridge in the background.*

*Right: the bridge as a
tableau of religious cer-
emony in 1932. Cardinal
Lorenzo Lauri made
the closing address of the
Eucharistic Congress from
O'Connell Bridge to an
estimated gathering of one
million people.*

Above: the wide sweep of O'Connell Bridge, looking north. O'Connell Street's notable landmarks can be seen in the background: the eponymously-named statue, the GPO and the Spire of Dublin.

Left: the solid stone of Dublin's most important bridge, gateway to O'Connell Street, the principal thoroughfare of the city.

Below: decorative facing on a pier.

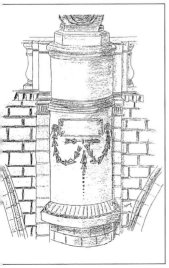

The Structure

O'Connell Bridge is a masonry, three-elliptical-arch bridge spanning the Liffey between O'Connell Street to the north and Westmoreland and D'Olier Streets to the south. It carries road and pedestrian traffic and will accomodate northbound light rail traffic. O'Connell Bridge has a total span of 45 metres and the width is 50 metres. A wide island runs across the bridge.

Construction of the present bridge began in 1877. Longitudinal north-south sections were first built on either side of an older structure, the Carlisle Bridge. The piers were based on riveted iron cylindrical caissons, which were slowly sunk excavating out river silt until founded on solid rock. The caissons were then filled with concrete and connected to the piers of the old bridge.

Abutment extensions were also necessary and these were founded on piles and concrete and built inside cofferdams. The elliptical arches were then built, springing between concrete-filled caisson and abutment. On completion in 1879 the side additions were opened for traffic. The superstructure of the old bridge was then removed and rebuilt to match the extensions.

The arches, arch rings, spandrels and lower piers are of well-cut granite ashlar, evenly coursed, while the parapet and greater part of the piers are of sandstone. While the parapets are simple – each is composed of eight sections of balusters, alternating with eight dadoes, four small and four large – the piers are rusticated and decorated. There are two keystones, also of sandstone, one on each central arch: a representation of Anna Livia looks to the west and one of the Atlantic Ocean looks eastwards. The keystones were designed by Charles V. Harrison.

The ornamental lamp standards were made in the Du Val d'Osne foundry in Paris. The shades are decorated with the Dublin Corporation motif and crowned with openwork palmettes and anthemions. Each shaft is decorated with volutes, rosettes, acanthus and lion heads while each base is embellished with bull-rushes and wild flowers, pateras and egg-and-dart motifs. In 2008, repairs necessitated by weather and water erosion to the pillars and balustrades were undertaken by Dublin City Council.

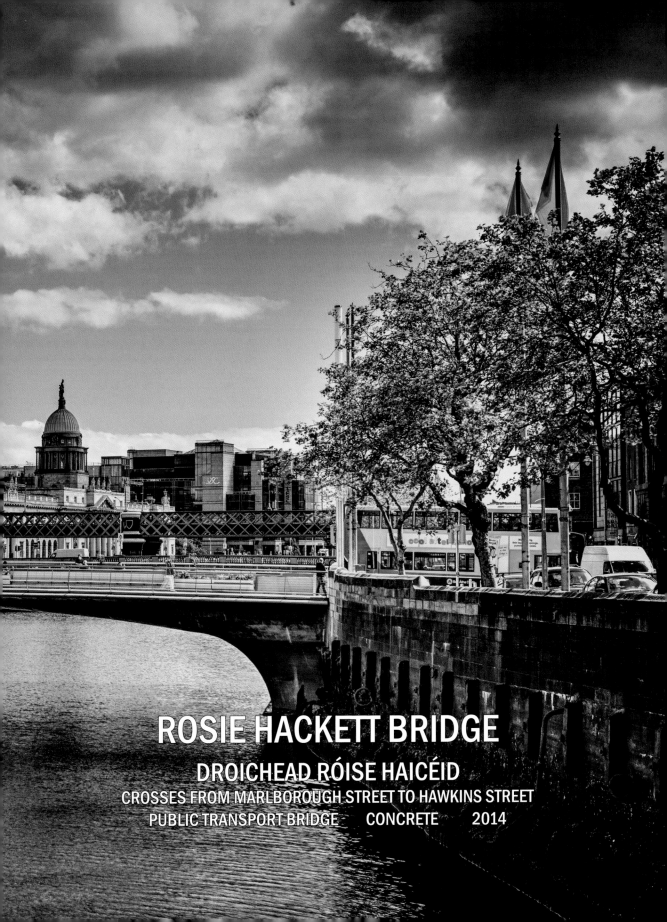

ROSIE HACKETT BRIDGE

DROICHEAD RÓISE HAICÉID
CROSSES FROM MARLBOROUGH STREET TO HAWKINS STREET
PUBLIC TRANSPORT BRIDGE   CONCRETE   2014

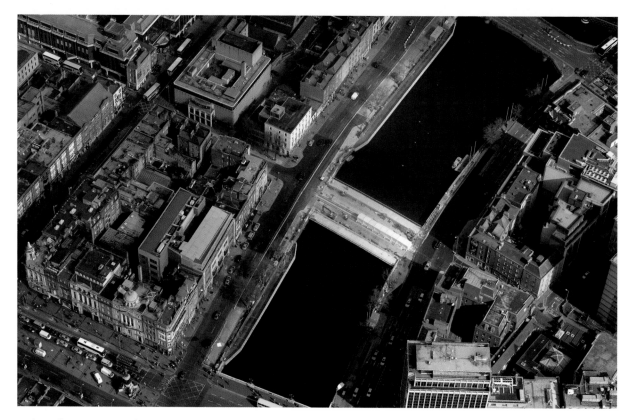

At the ceremonial opening of the Rosie Hackett Bridge, on 20th May 2014, an old Dublin tram emblazoned with a banner urging votes for women took pride of place. The significance is simple: the bridge is Dublin's first ever purpose-built bridge giving priority to public transport. It is currently the only Liffey bridge to be named for a woman – one who fought for women's rights. Rosie Hackett also took part in the 1916 Rising.

Above: new bridge on the block, the Rosie Hackett Bridge.

In February 2012 the appearance of a barge crane in the Liffey marked the beginning of the construction phase though planning of the bridge had begun long before that. 'Transport 21' and the 'Regional Planning Guidelines' all informed the decision to build this new bridge, in particular the City Council's 'Dublin City Development Plan 2011-2017' which contained a specific objective to provide a pedestrian bridge from Marlborough Street to Hawkins Street. Preliminary work included: land ownership searches, a topographical survey and consultations with utility companies, the National Parks and Wildlife Service, the Eastern Regional Fisheries Board and National Museum of Ireland. Archaeological testing and archaeological excavation were undertaken as were underwater assessments and metal detection surveys. An Environmental Impact Statement was also commissioned.

Below: at the opening of the new bridge that carries the Luas – an old Dublin tram.

Protecting the area from any future flooding was of major concern. A hydraulic model of the Liffey was developed and the impact of the new bridge under various combinations of low and high tide was tested.

Requirements for contractors were also set out: the use only of chemicals that were approved for the aquatic environment, noise control measures,

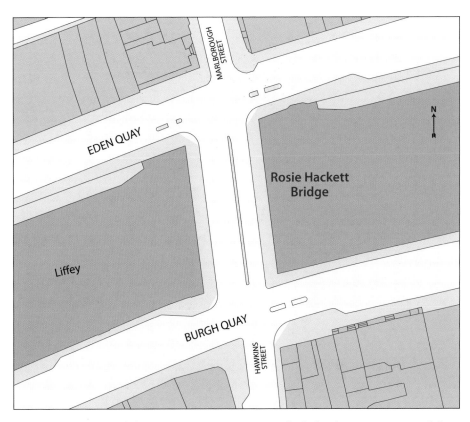

vibration limits and dust minimisation were included. Photomontages of the proposed structure were analysed for landscape and visual impact.

Method statements were prepared for the relocation of the Sheahan monument – a memorial to Patrick Sheahan, a member of the Dublin Metropolitan Police – and the temporary interference with parts of the historic quay walls.

The bridge is simple in design and sensitive to its surroundings – a low-arched, single-span, concrete structure complementing its classically elegant upstream neighbour, O'Connell Bridge – and is minimally intrusive upon the surrounding historic quayside and the river itself. Visually this is aided by the openwork balustrading, the shallow curve of the bridge soffit and the fluid continuation through to the connecting streets – Marlborough Street on the north side and Hawkins Street on the south. Technically this was achieved through the use of high-strength structural concrete which allowed aesthetic and geometrical flexibility and also provides robustness and longevity. The gentle rising abutment supports are also as unobtrusive as possible. Conservation of the protected quay walls and the historic area generally was ensured by the services of a specialist architect.

Tall poles provide a portal-like entrance for traffic onto and off the bridge. There are dedicated bus and taxi lanes, a cycle track and a *Luas* light rail corridor. There are two wide pedestrian walkways. For those who wish to linger and admire the riverscape there is seating formed from the concrete upstands, which separate pedestrians from road traffic and also function as flood de-

fences. Greenery softens and brightens the seating areas. At night, lighting, integrated into the seating, balustrades, handrails and portal poles, sets a contemporary scene.

Unobtrusive as the Rosie Hackett Bridge is on the riverscape, it, like every other Liffey bridge, performs a social and economic function. In this way it is very much a bridge of change. Pedestrians previously had to cross by the nearby O'Connell Bridge – the busiest walking route in the country. Now, a little to the east, they can cross on this new bridge, where once a ferry boat operated, (recorded in 1675). The bridge will also assist in the regeneration of the areas around Marlborough and Hawkins Streets.

Change too came with the naming of the bridge. Though many Liffey bridges have been christened formally and informally by Dubliners, for the first time ever suggestions were actively sought from individuals and groups – many were received. On 2nd September 2013, Dublin City Council, having whittled down the list, voted to name the Liffey's newest bridge after Rosie Hackett.

Above: ready for traffic. The bridge accommodates two bus lanes, a Luas track, a cycle track and two pedestrian walkways. The decorative bridge portals are designed to support the catenary for the Luas system.

Below: special grooved tram rails, being prepared for insertion in the bridge surface.

Above: much thought was given to ensuring that the the bridge was a place for pedestrians to linger and contemplate the river scene. The seating is formed by concrete upstands, which also function as flood defences. The greenery of the planters softens and brightens the seating areas.

Born in 1892, Rosie had once lived in a tenement on Old Abbey Street, just a stone's throw from where the bridge stands today. By age 19 she was an active member of the fledgling Irish Transport and General Workers' Union and agitated for better working conditions for her fellow women workers in the Jacob's biscuit factory. Having lost her job in the bitterly-fought Lockout labour dispute of 1913, she retrained as a printer. She also joined the Irish Citizen Army and saw action in 1916 at the College of Surgeons with Countess Markievicz and Michael Mallin. Released from Kilmainham Gaol, she refocused her considerable talents into re-forming the Irish Women Workers' Union and served the trade union movement for the rest of her working life.

Plaques in English and Irish commemorate the opening of the bridge, to which members of Rosie Hackett's family were invited. The plaque reads: Rosie Hackett Bridge; Opened 20th May 2014 by Oisín Quinn, Lord Mayor of Dublin; Michael Phillips, City Engineer; John W. Flanagan, Engineer for the project; Designed by Roughan and O'Donovan, Consulting Engineers; Seán Harrington, Architects; Constructed by Graham Projects Ltd.

Behind the simplicity of the bridge form and shape lies a lot of complexity. Above: protected by a sheet-pile dam, work proceeds on the shuttering to encase the concrete of an abutment – it is shaped as a double curve to allow the river to flow easily around it.

Left: in every era, advanced construction methods of the time have been used in the building of Liffey bridges. Here, steel reinforcing strands are being post-tensioned, a technique that allows for a more minimal structural depth.

Above: construction continued, day and night. Concrete pumps are used to make a large placement of concrete.

The Structure

The Rosie Hackett Bridge crosses the Liffey at a slight skew, connecting Marlborough Street on the north side to Hawkins Street on the south. It is an arched, single-span, concrete structure with a total length of 47 metres and a generous width of 26 metres. It is a public transport priority bridge accommodating dedicated bus and taxi lanes, a *Luas* light rail corridor, pedestrians and a cycle track. Integral flood protection walls or concrete upstands also serve as seating and provide planters for floral displays. The bridge has a gentle slope to ensure that it is user friendly. The openwork balustrading facilitates good views of the river.

The underside of the bridge has a shallow curve which tightens before reaching the quay walls to form the abutments, which are in the shape of a double curve on plan allowing the river to flow easily around them and limiting their protrusion into the river. The deck uses a combination of high-strength concrete and post-tensioning which allows for minimisation of the structural depth over the single span length.

Lighting is integrated into the seating, handrails and balustrades and is provided at the thresholds of the bridge from tall multi-functional poles: they also provide support for the *Luas* overhead wires.

Construction of the Rosie Hackett Bridge began in February 2012 and plaques, in English and Irish, commemorate the opening of the bridge on 20th May, 2014.

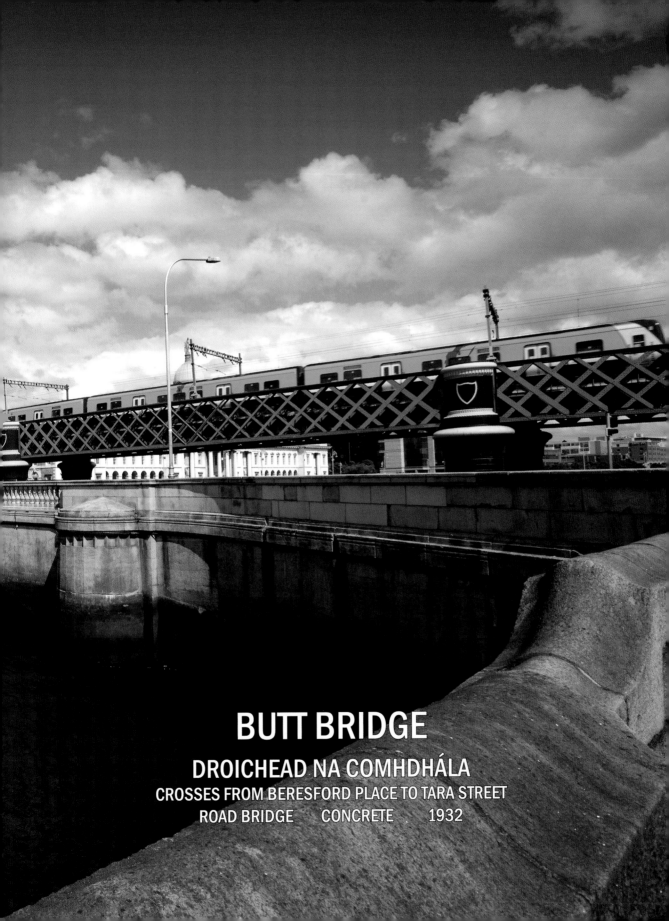

BUTT BRIDGE

DROICHEAD NA COMHDHÁLA
CROSSES FROM BERESFORD PLACE TO TARA STREET
ROAD BRIDGE   CONCRETE   1932

Butt Bridge can boast of a number of firsts. It was the first new bridge to cross the Liffey in the 20th century and was the first to use reinforced concrete as a building material. In its older guise, the Butt Bridge of 1879, it was the city's first swivel bridge.

The first steps towards the present day bridge were taken in 1925 when the Dublin Port and Docks Board lodged a bill for the reconstruction of the old bridge on this site. Their chief engineer, Joseph Mallagh, was given charge of the project. Several designs were considered but finance was tight – it was a time when the coffers of the newly independent Irish State had many competing claims. The reconstruction of architectural treasures such as the Custom House and the Four Courts (damaged in the conflicts of a decade before) had greater priority. A four-arched masonry design was rejected as cut stone was too costly and a metal structure was considered unsuitable given the proximity of the Loop Line Bridge which, many considered already sullied the view of the Custom House. Mallagh, with Pierce Purcell, consultant engineer, and O'Callaghan & Giron, Architects, thus designed the Liffey's first reinforced concrete bridge.

Work began in late 1930. A temporary bridge having been considered too problematic, vehicles were diverted to O'Connell Bridge where the rearrangement of the tram lines and a new system of traffic regulation facilitated the increased volumes. Pedestrians, however, were accommodated with a temporary crossing, made of light steel girders, supported on the piers of the Loop Line Bridge and resting on four timber trestles in the middle of the river.

On site the contractor had first to remove the old structure by cutting the ironwork into sections and lowering it onto barges. Masonry from the approach spans and piers was retained for use in the foundations of the new

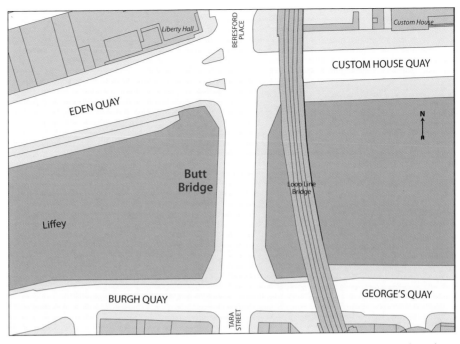

Right: map of the bridge area.

structure. These consisted of mass concrete bases and were constructed within a cofferdam of sheet steel piles.

The use of cofferdams, which enclose an underwater area which can then be pumped dry, was an innovative technique when first used on the Liffey by George Semple during the construction of his Essex Bridge in 1753.

Aligning the central span of the new bridge with the piers of the Loop Line Bridge downriver was essential for ease of navigation for river traffic. In addition, the bridge crosses the Liffey at a slight skew for a more efficient road traffic flow with Tara Street. To this end the bridge corners are also splayed. A roadway, 12 metres wide, and two footpaths, each 3.6 metres wide, are carried across the river on three spans which total 72 metres. The longer central span is 34 metres, while the individual approach spans each measure 12 metres. The simple parapets are of Ballyknockan granite.

A sense of urgency surrounded the completion of the bridge – an influx of visitors was expected for the 1932 Eucharistic Congress in Dublin thus the contract conditions stipulated a heavy penalty for any time overrun. On 25th May 1932 the bridge was tested using road rollers, steam wagons and lorries and declared officially open on 7th June. Despite delays, including that of six weeks due to a construction mishap, completion was ahead of time, earning the contractor, Gray's Ferro Concrete a bonus. The cost of the structure was £53,740.

The Congress was a great success. The view from the bridge on those June summer evenings was the sight of a lifetime for Dubliners. To the west the city was bedecked with garlands, flags, flowers and banners. Churchmen from faraway places, clad in exotic vestments, paraded on the streets. At night, the most modern lighting technology, then available, bathed Dublin's principal buildings in serene colours while to the east were the lights of numerous lin-

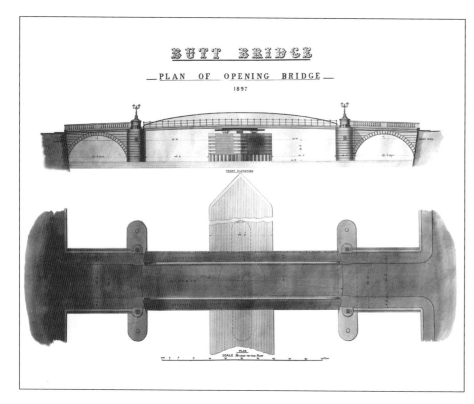

BUTT BRIDGE

PLAN OF OPENING BRIDGE

1897

FRONT ELEVATION

PLAN

SCALE 16 INCH TO THE FOOT

Left: the design plans of the 1879 Butt Bridge.

Below left: work is underway on the central swing span.

Below: the pioneering engineer of the Dublin Port and Docks Board, Bindon Blood Stoney. He was responsible for the construction of many bridges over the Liffey, including Grattan, O'Connell and Butt Bridges. In the late 19th century, during the great expansion of Dublin port, he devised an innovative lifting arrngement to place giant precast concrete blocks to form the city quay walls. The diving bell, used to prepare the surface of the river bed (an alternative to the caisson system), is now on permanent display at Sir John Rogerson's Quay.

CUSTOM HOUSE & SWIVEL BRIDGE DUBLIN 895. W..

Above: an historic photograph of the Custom House. The recently-constructed Butt Bridge is in the foreground. Arguably, it was a finer (albeit narrower) bridge than the concrete structure that replaced it. This downriver view of the Custom House is no longer possible, due to the construction of the intervening Loop Line Bridge of 1891.

ers berthed in Alexandra Basin, Scotsman's Bay and along Sir John Rogerson's Quay.

The older bridge had been named for Isaac Butt, the 'Father of Home Rule'. A one-time Tory conservative turned nationalist hero, his political movement dominated and defined Irish and British politics even after his death in 1879. Dublin Corporation proposed that the new bridge be named 'Congress Bridge'. However this was at a time other Liffey bridges were being renamed for Irish heroes of the past. A compromise saw a plaque, recording the 31st International Eucharistic Congress of 1932, being placed on the bridge, which retained the title, Butt Bridge.

Designed by Bindon Blood Stoney (the pioneering engineer of Dublin Port and Docks Board) the older structure here dated from 1879. That bridge was integral to the reconstruction of O'Connell Bridge (also designed by Stoney) and the management of the cross-river traffic in the immediate area. Stoney's design was of fixed masonry approach spans, each just over 11 metres long, and a central, rotating, cast-iron span of 38 metres manufactured by the Skerne Ironworks Company of Darlington. This swivel section allowed shipping access upstream and was powered by a 15-horsepower steam engine, each quarter turn marked by the peal of a bell. Two men and a winch were on standby if the steam engine should fail. The Swivel Bridge, as Dubliners liked

175

to call it, had a roadway width of a mere 5.6 metres, from which pedestrians were separated by iron railings. The approach gradient was steep and the thresholds narrow.

The total cost of construction was £44,663 6s 11d and the contractor was W.J. Doherty – who also built O'Connell Bridge. The very first vehicle to cross was that of Mrs Doherty at 11:20 am on 26th August 1879. In a two-week period shortly after it opened over 75,000 pedestrians, 2,200 cattle, 384 horse-riders and 38,000 carriages and drays were recorded as having used the bridge. Such a volume of traffic demonstrated the need for a river crossing here.

However, in 1888, the swivel section was decommissioned – the annual operating cost of £72 not being sufficiently matched by shipping dues for the upstream berths around O'Connell Bridge. For almost another half century the first Butt Bridge served Dubliners though as time progressed calls for its replacement grew louder. With an increased population and the grow-ing dominance of motor vehicles the narrow, hump backed 19th-century bridge was not fit for purpose. It closed on the 1st December 1930. The two manifestations of Butt Bridge, Stoney's Victorian iron bridge and Mallagh's 20th-century concrete structure were the most easterly road crossings over the Liffey for 99 years. That honour was lost to the Talbot Memorial Bridge when, in 1978, it opened downstream.

Above: new lighting installed on the bridge in 2015.

The Structure

The present 20th-century Butt Bridge is a three span bridge connecting Beresford Place on the north side to Tara Street on the south. The middle span is formed by two cast in-situ reinforced cantilevers from the approach spans and dowelled longitudinally at mid span. It was the first reinforced concrete bridge to be built across the Liffey. It crosses the river at a slight skew with a central span of 34 metres and approach spans of 12 metres each. A fixed river navigation channel for small craft was ensured by aligning the central span with the piers of the Loop Line Bridge downstream. Road traffic and pedestrians are accommodated on the 12 metre wide roadway and two footpaths, each of 3.6 metres. The total width of the bridge across the spandrels on the central span is 20 metres.

The foundations for the piers and abutments consist of mass concrete bases in which large stones from the previous bridge were placed and were constructed within a cofferdam of sheet steel piles. The piers and abutments were constructed in two stages: first the north pier and abutment in one large cofferdam, while the south side was built using two cofferdams.

The cantilevers are of cellular reinforced concrete on mass concrete piers, balanced by solid reinforced concrete approach spans and abutments. The central and approach spans are integral with the pier. The parapets over the central span consist of an open balustrade of Ballyknockan granite, interspersed with dadoes.

A series of tunnels are housed within the bridge, some up to two metres in height and are used for the inspection of the mains services carried across the bridge.

O'Callaghan & Giron were the architects. The engineers were Joseph Mallagh of the Port and Docks Board with Pierce Purcell, consultant. The contractors were Gray's Ferro Concrete Ltd. The total cost was £65,500. Butt Bridge officially opened on the 7th June 1932.

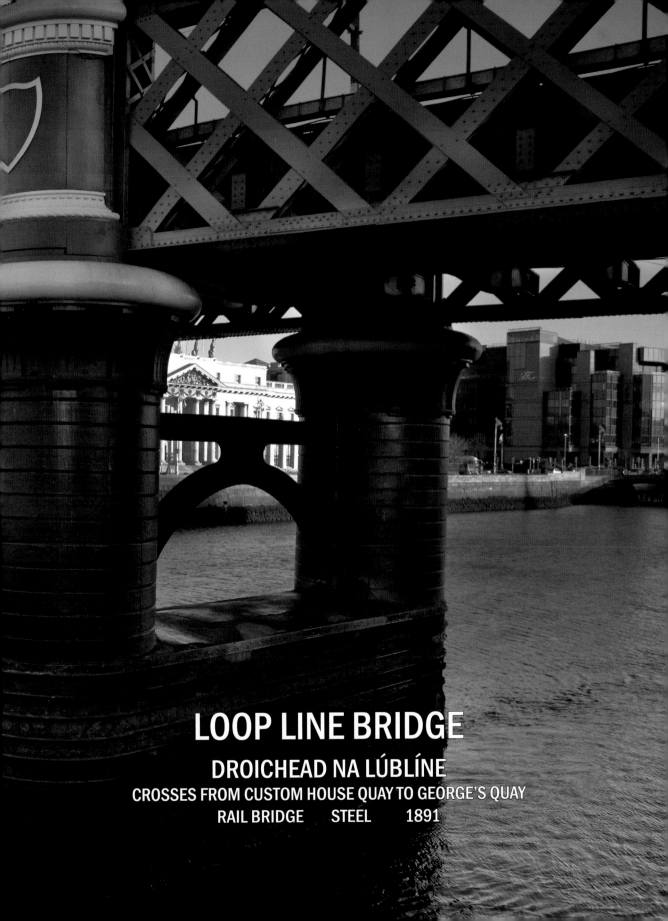

LOOP LINE BRIDGE

DROICHEAD NA LÚBLÍNE
CROSSES FROM CUSTOM HOUSE QUAY TO GEORGE'S QUAY
RAIL BRIDGE STEEL 1891

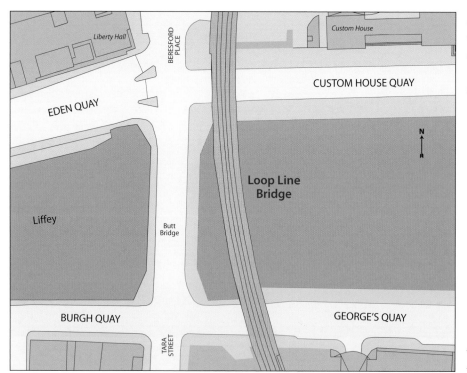

Left: map of the Loop Line Bridge area.

The Loop Line Bridge has always excited controversy. At the heart of the matter is that it obscures a view of Gandon's Custom House, that regally commands the north bank of the river, the finest 18th-century building in Dublin.

When first proposed by the railways and debated in the British Parliament, the building of the bridge was adamantly opposed by the Dublin representatives who pleaded that the view of the Custom House was the only thing left to the Irish since the passing of the Act of Union. Although better access by railway to Kingstown would result in a more efficient cross-channel mail service, Belfast politicians disliked that the northern mail would be routed through Dublin. Dublin Corporation opposed it too as did the Port and Docks Board who demanded £30,000 in compensation as ships would no longer be able to navigate upstream. Letter writers to the *Freeman's Journal* and the *Irish Times* suggested moving the bridge eastwards with one reader stoutly declaring the bridge 'an act of vandalism' upon the city. Their words fell on deaf ears. During the planning phase, in an effort to defuse the opposition, a white-painted, wooden model of the bridge was erected in nearby Beresford Place. A strip of yellow tape was placed across a photograph of the Custom House to illustrate the visual impact. The railways prevailed and in due course the Loop Line Act of 1884 was passed.

Construction commenced in September 1889 to a design by John Chaloner Smith, engineer to the Dublin, Wicklow and Wexford Railway. The bridge is typical (and has the heaviness) of many late-Victorian railway bridges. Deep lattice-girder beams are located on each side and support the bridge deck. The lattice girders were of steel (steel was displacing wrought iron by this time)

CUSTOM HOUSE.DUBLIN. 710.W.L.

and these were fabricated by William Arrol of Glasgow. The bridge is supported by a double row of cylindrical, cast-iron piers in the river with two further piers on the north bank near the Custom House. The three spans are of different lengths: 38, 40 and 39 metres.

Efforts were made to blend in the bridge with its surroundings. The piers have a ringed appearance, mimicking courses of masonry. The piers on the approach viaduct by Beresford Place were of stone. Classical columns were provided with carved decoration on top.

By October 1890, the bridge was almost ready and the contractors, M. Mead and Sons of Dublin, did not waste time. They set up their stall on the quayside to auction off 420 logs of the best red and pitch pine timber and another 800 pieces of pine deal, parcelled in lots of 20. The timber, which had been used for shoring of the bridge during the period of construction, was no longer required. Advertisements appeared shortly afterwards in the *Free-*

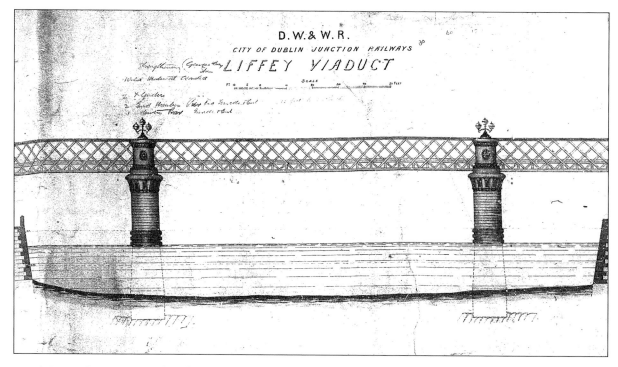

D. W. & W. R.

CITY OF DUBLIN JUNCTION RAILWAYS

LIFFEY VIADUCT

SCALE

Above: construction drawing. Side elevation of the planned railway bridge over the Liffey.

man's Journal inviting tenders for the painting of the bridge with two coats of Champion Paint.

Transport and communication were key to industrial development during Victorian times. The Loop Line was a vital part of a two kilometre-long link between the great railway lines of 19th-century Ireland: the northern line, operated by the Great Northern Railway (also connected via the Phoenix Park to the Great Southern and Western Railway to the south and west) and the rail services through south Dublin and beyond to Wexford, operated by the Dublin, Wicklow and Wexford Railway.

When the Loop Line, or City of Dublin Junction Railways connection, was opened in 1891, it allowed the London mails arriving from Holyhead to Kingstown (Dún Laoghaire), to be transported directly by train to Belfast and also to Cork. Previously mails were put on horse-drawn carts to transfer to Amiens Street, Broadstone or Kingsbridge stations. In addition, Atlantic steamers called at Queenstown to pick up and set down mails for Great Britain which would be now conveyed via Kingstown and Holyhead as it was faster than waiting for the ships to reach Southampton.

Over the century and a quarter since its opening, ideas have surfaced from time to time for the replacement or enhancement of the Loop Line Bridge. Dublin Corporation in the 1920s explored the feasibility of replacing the bridge with a rail tunnel under the Liffey. This idea surfaced again in 1967, though as far back as 1864 two shafts had been sunk in the river and a tunnel declared impossible. Converting the space under the archways of the bridge into air raid shelters was suggested in 1941. In the early 1970s disguising the bridge with a painted mural was a topic of conversation while a brave politician promised in 1973 that the Loop Line would blight the Dublin landscape

184

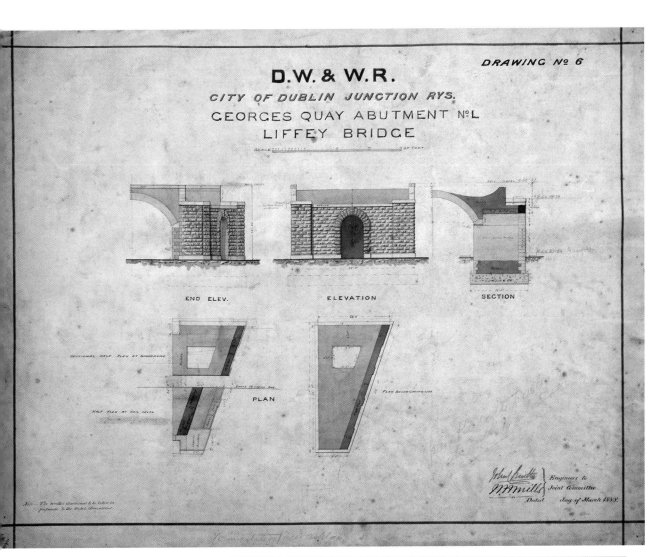

D.W. & W.R.
CITY OF DUBLIN JUNCTION RYS.
GEORGES QUAY ABUTMENT Nº L
LIFFEY BRIDGE

DRAWING Nº 6

END ELEV.   ELEVATION   SECTION

PLAN

Above: Victorian engineering drawings, with their use of watercolour, are veritable works of art. Drawing of George's Quay abutment for the Loop Line Bridge.

The Dublin, Wicklow and Wexford Railway was renamed the Dublin and South Eastern Railway (DSER) in 1906. Right: insignia of the DSER.

for a mere five years more. In 1993 the Institute of Engineers of Ireland held a competition for its replacement. The winning design, by Kavanagh, Mansfield and Bullen, was costed at £1.8 million but only ever built in model form. The appearance of the bridge was much improved following the decision in 2004 to remove unsightly advertising billboards.

The bridge has won its place in Dublin's history – it was witness to the action by the gunship *Helga* during Easter 1916. Moored just by the Custom House, it shelled Liberty Hall through the spaces under the bridge, between the piers. Accounts say that the ship's opening shot hit the Loop Line Bridge. In 1921, when the Custom House was burned during the War of Independence, much of the action took place under and around the bridge.

The bridge has also been called the Liffey Viaduct. Disputed as it was and still is, it has yet found a place in Dublin lore, even inspiring a reference in James Joyce's Ulysses: 'A skiff, a crumpled throwaway, Elijah is coming, rode lightly down the Liffey, under Loopline Bridge, shooting the rapids where water chafed around the bridgepiers, sailing eastward past hulls and anchorchains, between the Customhouse old dock and George's quay.'

Above; a receding pattern of steel cross girders, from the Loop Line Bridge. Rehabiliation of these was carried out in the period 1958-60 at the Inchicore Railway Works.

Right: in the aftermath of the burning of the Custom House in 1921, British soldiers, with a Peerless armoured car monitor civilians by the bridge. From the shelling of Liberty Hall in 1916, to the War of Independence, the Loop Line Bridge has framed many scenes of 20th-century history.

Left: a double row of circular cast-iron piers. The piers were solidly founded, being sunk through approximately three metres of river mud and gravel where they are anchored onto rock by means of centre dowels which extend into the hard layer.

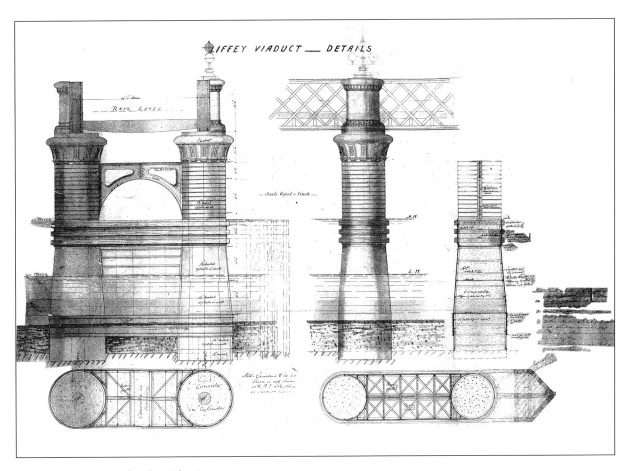

Above: construction detail of the piers.

The Structure

The Loop Line Bridge (also known as the Liffey Viaduct) is a three-span, steel lattice-girder bridge which carries two rail lines of sharply-curved ballasted track across the Liffey, above Custom House Quay on the north side and George's Quay on the south, at around six metres above road level.

A double row of braced, cast-iron piers support the bridge over the river, the cylindrical members being hollow and constructed, in a series of six vertical levels, as caissons. They were sunk through approximately three metres of river mud and gravel where they are anchored onto rock by means of centre dowels which extend 1.5 metres into the hard layer. The top three sections are three metres diameter tapering from 4.2 metre diameter sections. The uppermost parts of the cylinders are topped by ornamented sections which carry the main lattice girders. The viaduct section on the north side rests on faux-granite white limestone piers.

The total span length is 117 metres, the three straight spans being of different lengths: 38, 40 and 39 metres. The cross-girders originally carried a steel trough deck, however, due to deterioration these were replaced between 1958 and 1960.

The bridge (now designated Underbridge No. 43, Dublin-Wexford line) was commissioned by the Dublin, Wicklow and Wexford Railway and designed by its engineer, John Chaloner Smith. It opened in 1891.

TALBOT MEMORIAL BRIDGE

DROICHEAD CUIMHNEACHÁIN AN TALBÓIDIGH

CROSSES FROM MEMORIAL ROAD TO MOSS STREET

ROAD BRIDGE   CONCRETE   1978

The Talbot Memorial Bridge provides an important road crossing over the river from Custom House Quay and Memorial Road on the north bank to City Quay and Moss Street on the south.

The bridge is modest in style and appearance. Yet it has garnered some firsts. When construction started on this, it was 46 years since the city had seen major bridge work across the Liffey – the last being when the 19th-century swivel Butt Bridge was replaced with Dublin's first reinforced concrete bridge in 1932. The construction of the bridge here resulted in another step-change in the riverscape. Ships could no longer moor by Gandon's 18th-century Custom House. The Talbot Memorial Bridge was now the Liffey's most easterly bridge, a position once held by Butt Bridge. In engineering 'firsts' it was the first Liffey bridge to use pre-stressed concrete as a structural medium.

Work began in June 1976. People passing by the construction site could observe workers not labouring merely by the river but actually in it too, assembling a seemingly chaotic collection of steel girders, wooden piles and concrete slabs into a slimline, simple three-span bridge rendered softer on the eye by a surface sprinkling of Wicklow and Scottish granite dust on the external structure. To minimise the obstruction to the river flow, the reinforced concrete piers are also of a slender design. The project – a welcome side effect of which was to increase economic activity in the area – took a mere 20 months to complete and on 14th February 1978, the first official crossing took place.

Once open, the Talbot Memorial Bridge fulfilled the planners' intentions – diverting traffic away from O'Connell and Butt Bridges and to the lesser-used traffic lanes in this – at the time – much quieter eastern quarter. The city traffic problems had been of great concern with studies confirming what the motorist had long experienced – that the traffic volume had increased by 50% over a ten-year period while the number of cars in the greater Dublin area had increased three-fold since the 1950s. The existing Liffey bridge network was

Right: map of bridge

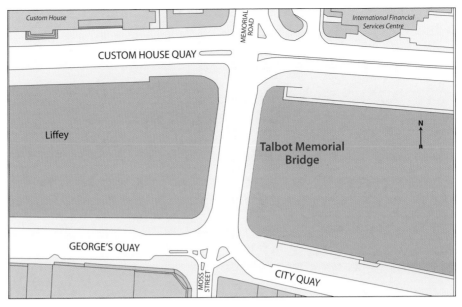

barely coping and some – O'Connell and Butt Bridges –were near capacity. The new bridge and its westerly partner, the Frank Sherwin Bridge which opened four years later in 1982, facilitated vehicles travelling in a circular movement up and down the quays thus optimising the overall traffic flow.

Perhaps nowhere else along the long course of the Liffey through the city is the 'then and now' so utterly stark as here by the Talbot Memorial Bridge. Once this area was a run down and mostly forgotten backwater. Now it is an eclectic urban landscape of the old and the new. This workaday and understated bridge rests low in the river, complementing the adjacent office blocks of concrete and glass, yet all the while allowing the historic and architecturally unique Custom House to retain its pride of place, pre-eminent on the riverscape.

Many proposals were received by Dublin Corporation for the naming of the bridge and in the end a compromise was reached and the bridge was named for heroic Dubliners. One such was Matthew Talbot. Born in 1856, he was another luckless tenement child born in yet another Dublin slum not so very far from the bridge which today bears his name. It seemed as if his story would be the same as many other young men from Dublin's neglected inner city – to work hard when work could be got, live harder and die tragically young.

Below: driving to solid foundations – a plentitude of piles.

From somewhere Talbot found, at the age of 28, the strength to change his path in life. He turned away from alcohol and instead found sustenance in prayer. Life continued as hard as ever before and Talbot lived through the conflict of the early 20th century including the Lockout of 1913. He bore witness to the Easter Rising of 1916, the War of Independence and the Civil War. Throughout all he lived a life of piety and asceticism.

He died on a Dublin street one morning in June 1925. His story of devotion and charity became known and passed from neighbour to neighbour, county to county and even from country to country. In 1975 he was declared

'venerable' by Pope Paul VI and is a patron of those struggling with alcoholism. His statue stands on the south end of the bridge.

Though Talbot never ventured far from the city streets so familiar to him, other working class youths from Dublin city and beyond found the call of the sea irresistible. They lived, worked and died on the high seas fishing for a living or in the service of merchant marines around the world. During the course of World War II they manned the boats which braved the seas, in peril of being torpedoed, bringing much needed supplies home at a time of dire shortages. 136 Irish seamen died, the last such tragedy being on 2nd May 1945, when three crew members of the trawler *Naomh Garbhan* fell victim to a torpedo picked up in their fishing net.

The Talbot Memorial Bridge, like many other Liffey bridges, stands as a monument to uncommon men and women of times past.

Above: with the Busárus in the background, a scene during construction. Two pre-stressed precast concrete beams have been laid in position.

The Structure

The Talbot Memorial Bridge is a three-span, pre-stressed concrete bridge crossing from Memorial Road on the north side to Moss Street on the south. The centre span is 34 metres and the side spans are each 22 metres. Interlocking steel sheet piling was used to form the cofferdams – some difficulties were experienced in sealing and drying out these. Precast pre-stressed concrete beams were placed on the piers. The pre-stressed beams were post-tensioned in a two stage stressing operation. The structure was completed with an in-situ reinforced concrete deck.

The slender, reinforced concrete piers are founded on a very deep stratum of hard calp limestone. Stabilisation and strengthening of the river wall at the south abutment was necessary. This was done with reinforced concrete, overlaid with a capping beam which carries the bridge bearing. At the north abutment the bridge bearing consists of a reinforced concrete pile cap, carried by a system of reinforced concrete piles.

The superstructure consists of eleven precast I-shaped beams which are of varying section with thickening of the webs over the supports. These are clad with precast concrete panels, surface treated by acid etching with Wicklow and Scottish granite dust – a process developed especially for use on this bridge. During construction the central beams were first lifted onto a barge at the quayside. The barge was towed into mid-river and the beams were craned into place.

The Talbot Memorial Bridge was designed by L. F. Stephens of De Leuw, Chadwick and O'hEocha, the contractors were Ascon Ltd and the final cost was £1.05 million.

SEÁN O'CASEY BRIDGE

DROICHEAD SHEÁIN UÍ CHATHASAIGH

CROSSES FROM CUSTOM HOUSE QUAY TO CITY QUAY

PEDESTRIAN BRIDGE STEEL 2005

Travelling downstream, the Seán O'Casey Bridge, a steel structure of distinctive styling, is the last of the trio of pedestrian-only bridges over the Liffey within the city. This modern structure is a steel bridge of distinctive styling. For those travelling upstream it is the last of the trio of opening bridges – ships must first navigate through the concrete East-Link, then the futuristic Samuel Beckett before each 44 metre arm of the Seán O'Casey Bridge swings open into a parallel formation, to allow vessels to proceed along the river channel.

The bridge, connecting Custom House Quay on the north bank to City Quay on the south, was commissioned by the Dublin Docklands Development Authority which had statutory responsibility for regeneration of this once-rundown, neglected but historic city district.

From a watery wasteland, a streetscape began to emerge here from the turn of the 18th century. The quay walls were built – City Quay on the south bank is a recorded industrial heritage monument – and people moved in to settle in this area. Businesses grew up with many of their activities focussed on the river and its shipping industry.

In the 19th century this was a vibrant area thronged with seafarers, hawkers, barefoot children and dray horses hauling carts along the cobbled streets. Music, conversation and the occasional brawl spilled out from the pubs. Ferries shuttled across the river and ships' sails cluttered the skyline. The shippers and merchants grew prosperous as each cargo of sugar, tobacco or whiskey was unloaded into the dockside warehouses. However, poverty and disease ran unchecked in the back streets and lanes.

Above: pedestrian in function, but definitely not in form, the Seán O'Casey Bridge briskly cuts across the river.

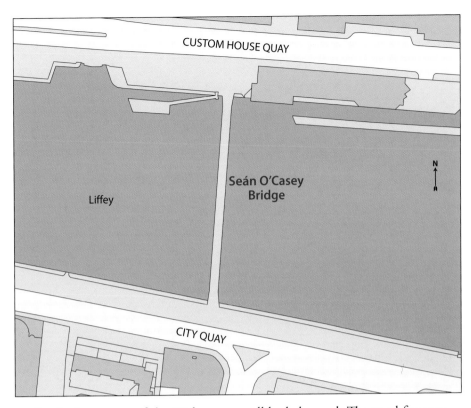

By the latter part of the 20th century all had changed. The need for storage facilities and unloading areas was drastically reduced with the advent of container cargo and roll-on roll-off ferries. Sites became derelict and jobs disappeared. The population of the Docklands area halved between 1900 and the 1980s with many of those remaining suffering poor living conditions.

A first step towards regeneration of the area came with the 1986 Urban Renewal Act. Then in 1987 the International Financial Services Centre was set up on the north bank of the river. In 1997 the Dublin Docklands Development Authority was established by statute and charged with tackling the economic and social decline of the area as a whole. One of the many initiatives undertaken was the development of a new bridge. The intention for this bridge was not only to connect the social and business communities but also as a means to encourage integration into the wider city.

A design competition was organised. From 80 international entries the winning design team was selected and appointed by December 2002. Within a 30 month period all licences, environmental impact studies and legal consents were sought, granted and the bridge was constructed.

The Seán O'Casey Bridge utilises a pioneering swing action which sees the two leaves or arms of the bridge rotate on central bearings supported on granite clad piers in the river. Each leaf is 44 metres long and weighs around 160 tonnes.

A series of innovative floating horizontal tubes with buoyancy boxes, supported and guided on vertical piles anchored in the river protect the structure from accidental damage by passing boats.

A truly pan-European project, the opening section was made in Britain as was the balustrade, the deck was made in Denmark, the balustrade panels came from France, some construction took place in Poland and the stone originated in Ireland.

The design by Brian O'Halloran, Architects and O'Connor Sutton Cronin, Consulting Engineers, received an RIAI award and the Institution of Structural Engineers Award for Pedestrian Bridges in 2006, and an International Architecture Award in 2007.

The bridge is one of three named for Dublin writers of international acclaim. Seán O'Casey (1880–1964) was brought up in the docklands on the north side. This Protestant rebel in a Catholic city was a one-time railway worker. A member of the Irish Republican Brotherhood, he was the General Secretary of the Irish Citizen Army. O'Casey also was involved with the fledgling Irish Transport and General Workers' Union. All the while he was, as he once wrote: "out listening to everything, looking at everything and thinking it all out afterwards". In his internationally famous plays, 'The Shadow of a Gunman', 'The Plough and the Stars' and 'Juno and the Paycock', Dublin featured centre stage.

Above: the structural steel of the Seán O'Casey Bridge, frames a downriver vista that includes the Samuel Beckett Bridge, the 'Jeanie Johnston' tall ship, and on the left, the tilting glass drum of the Convention Centre.

200

Above: towering over the river, a giant crane places the steel superstructure of the bridge.

Well over a 1,000 years ago, Danish longboats sailed upriver here on a mission to plunder. Right: in a far more serendipitous manner, the deck of the bridge, neatly fabricated in Danish structural steel, is towed upriver to form part of the Seán O'Casey Bridge.

O'Casey wrote: "I have lived a troublesome life in Ireland, in my youth hard times in the body, and in my manhood years, a hard time in the spirit". Even when living away from his native city, his relationship with it was a tempestuous one. "Drums of Father Ned", selected for the Dublin Theatre Festival in 1958, was withdrawn by him following intimations of disapproval by the influential Roman Catholic Archbishop of Dublin, John Charles Mc-Quaid. The playwright banned production of his plays in the Irish Republic for the rest of his life. He died in Torquay, England in 1964.

By day this cosmopolitan quarter now seethes with the energy of a youthful, purposeful population and those taking leisurely strolls along the tree-lined campshires. By night it is a reflective river of light. Markets and festivals bring occasional colourful vibrancy.

Dubliners have taken O'Casey's namesake bridge to their heart – a measure of which is to dub it with witty nicknames. For some it is the 'Bingo Bridge' allowing northsiders and southsiders to frequent each other's bingo halls. For others it is the 'Quiver in the River', inspired by the apparent bounce bridge users experience as they saunter across.

A plaque commemorates the opening of the Seán O'Casey Bridge on 13th July 2005 and gives Seán O'Casey himself the definitive last words:

"Take heart of grace from your city's hidden splendour".

Above: a view from the northern campshires. The Seán O'Casey Bridge is a three-span cantilever swing structure. Each balanced-cantilever bridge arm rotates about a bearing mechanism at the centre point of each pier.

Right: the bridge opened for river traffic.

The Structure

The Seán O'Casey Bridge is a three-span, cantilever (swing), pedestrian crossing connecting Custom House Quay to City Quay on the south side. The total span length is 97 metres.

The structural design of the bridge evolved on the basic principle of a balanced cantilever, where each bridge leaf or arm, 44 metres long, rotates about a bearing mechanism at the centre point of each pier and closes onto a cantilever abutment.

The 4.5 metre wide aluminium bridge deck is supported on two 600 mm diameter steel tubes which are subsequently supported at their extreme ends via 100 mm diameter tension rods. Separate rods extend continuously on each side, which are in turn tensioned down to the central cradle base. It weighs over 320 tonnes and sits on two granite piers (the abutments are also clad in granite). When closed to river traffic, each bridge leaf is both locked together and to the cantilever abutments via hydraulic locking pins.

The cradle base and slew ring bearing is supported on stone-clad elliptical concrete piers located approximately 27 metres from each quay wall. The concrete piers, supported on piles, were cast within a prefabricated steel caisson temporarily placed in the river during construction.

A hand-held pendant key controls the operation of the bridge. The locking pins are released by radio controlled signal to the hydraulic rams at each slew ring bearing. The electric controls and hydraulic system are suspended in the zone of main structure beneath the bridge deck.

The bridge is protected against collision by a series of floating horizontal tubes with buoyancy boxes, supported and guided on vertical piles. This system conceals the V-fenders at water level, which rise and fall with the tide.

The bridge, which opened on 13th July, 2005, was commissioned by the Dublin Docklands Development Authority. It was designed by O'Connor Sutton Cronin Consulting Engineers and Brian O'Halloran, Architects.

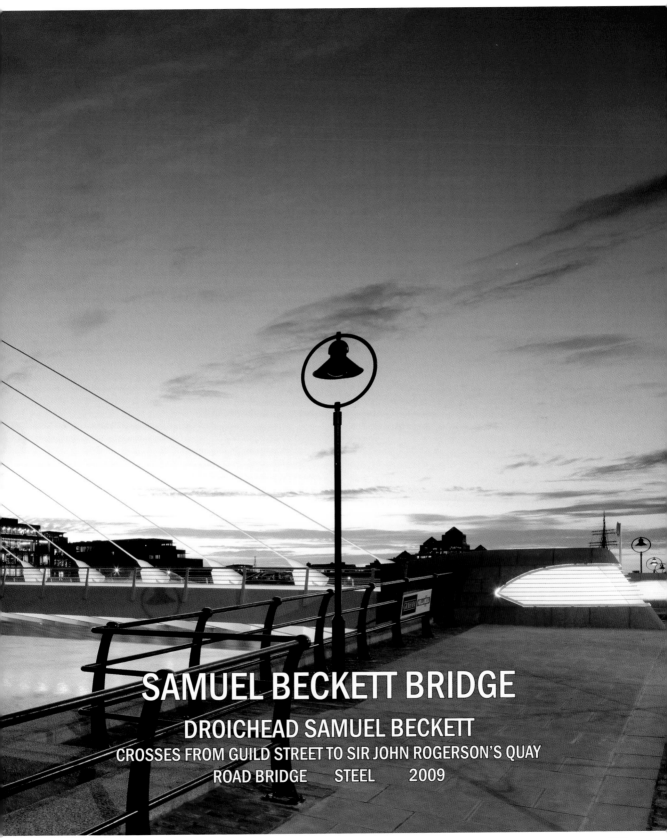

SAMUEL BECKETT BRIDGE

DROICHEAD SAMUEL BECKETT

CROSSES FROM GUILD STREET TO SIR JOHN ROGERSON'S QUAY

ROAD BRIDGE   STEEL   2009

In the history of Liffey bridges, spanning one thousand years and more, the
elegant and iconic Samuel Beckett is but a newcomer. It opened on 10th
December 2009 – yet it has already become an internationally-recognised
symbol of Dublin.

The genesis of the bridge project is to be found in the 1997 master plan
for the Dublin Docklands area – at that time a neglected quarter of the city
of boarded-up and dilapidated buildings, a stark symbol of urban decline.

The plan was simple, yet bold: the social and economic rebirth of the area.
Amongst several initiatives, there was a realisation that there needed to be an
equally bold physical manifestation – such as a statement bridge. The internationally renowned – and controversial – Spanish architect and engineer Santiago Calatrava was appointed in 1999. His vision for the Docklands bridge
came in a fleeting thought captured. As an Irish coin flipped through the air,
the embossed harp twisting and turning, Calatrava translated, pen onto paper.

This idea, a mere sketch at first, was presented to Dublin City Council,
who, in partnership with the Dublin Docklands Development Authority and
the Department of Environment, Heritage and Culture, was funding the
project. Its genius was instantly recognised.

In conjunction with the Irish consultants, Roughan and O'Donovan, Calatrava developed his inspired concept into a series of working drawings setting out in detail a functional bridge design. The planning process proceeded
and in 2000 an Environmental Impact Statement concluded that wildlife in
the area would not be adversely affected by the bridge, though some protective measures were needed to safeguard the swan, salmon and eel populations.

Right: map of the bridge.

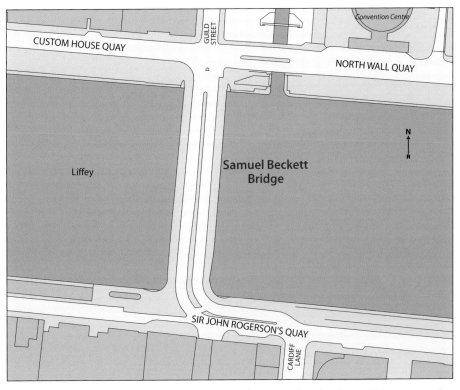

The bridge was constructed by the Graham Hollandia Joint Venture, with Graham working on the site from April 2007 in building the abutments, pivot pier and the necessary road works. Hollandia fabricating the single-span bridge deck in Rotterdam.

On 3rd May 2009, following a complex nine-hour operation involving a 160-wheeled truck and a sea-going barge, the superstructure of the Samuel Beckett Bridge was ready to depart Rotterdam. With many Rotterdammers looking on, the futuristic new bridge for Dublin, loaded on a sea-going barge, set sail on its 1,000 kilometre journey to Dublin.

Social media gave hourly updates on its progress: down the English Channel, around Land's End, up the Irish Sea along the east coast of Ireland and finally into Dublin Bay. Crowds gathered along the quaysides to give the new arrival a rousing *céad míle fáilte*.

Days later, in a meticulously-planned operation, the superstructure passed by the East-Link Bridge. Installation was precisely and cleverly planned, making best use of the natural forces of the river and tide: two barges shared the weight of the deck, the bridge pivot resting between them and above the water. At high tide the pivot was then floated over the base post onto which it settled as the tide ebbed.

Work continued apace including the completion of a high-specification, copper-roofed, control room building on Sir John Rogerson's Quay which is linked, via ducts placed along the river bed, to the bridge's hydraulic rotational mechanism housed in the main support pier.

Left: steel fabrication by Hollandia.

Left: work on the foundations of the circular pier. Within the cofferdam, piling is underway down to the underlying limestone.

The Samuel Beckett Bridge facilitates an environmental traffic cell strategy for the immediate area and for the quays as a whole. This allows orbital routes of the north and south sides to operate and link up.

The traffic lanes run in both directions across the single, 123 metre span of the bridge, one for general traffic and the other for buses. Cyclists and pedestrians are accommodated in dedicated lanes, also running in both directions. Crucially, this layout can be reconfigured to facilitate future tram lines.

For river traffic the Samuel Beckett is a gateway bridge, swinging to allow vessels to pass. Its 5,850 tonnes weight lifts 75 mm before rotating through 90 degrees. The base of the cable-stayed steel pylon is set safely outside the river's navigational channel. On closing, locking pins secure the bridge to the abutments.

The bridge embodies cutting-edge engineering techniques. It is a cable stayed, steel box-girder bridge, supported on capped, bored concrete piles which support a circular concrete pier. The bearings, two hydraulic push-pull cylinders and lifting equipment are housed in the circular concrete pivot pier.

Above: maritime man-ouevres – the steel pylon of the future Samuel Beckett Bridge is securely lifted by giant cranes in Rotterdam.

Right: in Rotterdam, the 160 wheels of this special truck support the super-structure as it is transported to the sea-going barge for its journey to Dublin.

The cable-stay design means that there is an enormous force on the back
cables – the equivalent of the weight of 80,000 people, the capacity of Croke
Park. Maintenance must be carried out on the rotating mechanism every
three months. The bridge is also opened every two weeks to keep it in good
condition. A series of tunnels, some large enough for a man to walk through,
facilitate internal maintenance.

It is not just advanced engineering – this bridge achieves the pinnacle
of aestheticism: there is a sleekness to the north curving pylon, its tip a
commanding 48 metres above the river. The ascending 25 cables evoke the
strings of a harp in sweet aeolian order. A quirky porthole displays the close
attention to fine finishes and detail. The neutral white colour slims the per-
ceived mass of the bridge, blends in with the skyline and complements the
contemporary architecture of the area.

The bridge was conceptually twinned with the James Joyce Bridge upriver: both are named after Irish literary giants; both are designed by Calatrava,
using his characteristic steel upperstructure, painted in white. Initially it had

Right: reflections. The bridge seamlessly blends with, and complements, the riverscape.

Right: the porthole frames the vessels of the Tall Ships Festival. Fine detail is evident all along this outstanding bridge.

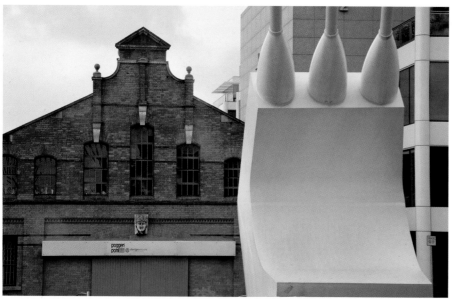

a working title of the Macken Street Bridge and in 2006 was formally named while still at design concept stage.

Samuel Beckett, a Dubliner, was born in 1906. From the affluent suburb of Foxrock, it looked as if his life was predetermined: to have a carefree childhood, attend good schools, study in university and enter the family business, picking up the necessary social graces and connections along the way. His privileged upbringing started as it should – he roamed the open countryside around his home in sight of the Dublin mountains and attended a select school. In Easter 1916 he spent his tenth birthday watching Dublin burn from the safe distance of the hills. At the age of 13 he was sent to Portora Royal boarding school in Enniskillen. Trinity College, Dublin was next, where he studied English, French and Italian.

Dublin of 1923 was a desolate place. There was economic stagnation following the turmoil of previous years. On completing his studies Samuel Beckett, the young man, rejected his predetermined fate. He taught, he travelled, he fought with his mother and lost his beloved father to a too-early death. He chose writing and left the destitution of Dublin for the sanctuary of Paris. Amongst the intellectual milieu, he befriended James Joyce. He had an intense relationship with Suzanne Deschevaux-Dumesnil, eventually marrying her. For his work in the French resistance during the Second World War, he received the *Croix de Guerre*.

Beckett's first published work of fiction, 'Assumption' appeared in 1929 and he was awarded his first literary prize, for the poem 'Whoroscope' the following year. His works include the trilogy of novels, 'Molloy', 'Malone Dies' and 'The Unnamable', and the plays 'Waiting for Godot' and 'Endgame'. He was awarded the Nobel Prize in 1969 "for his writing, which – in new forms for the novel and drama – in the destitution of modern man acquires its elevation". He died in Paris on 22nd December 1989 a mere five months after his wife.

Below: solid sentinels along the river. These fender-piles protect the Samuel Beckett Bridge from collision by vessels.

Right: a pleasing pattern — receding into the distance, the substantial anchor supports of the descending forestay cables.

The Structure

The Samuel Beckett Bridge is a cable-stayed, steel box-girder structure stretching from Guild Street on the north bank to Sir John Rogerson's Quay on the south in a single span of 123 metres.

The main concrete support in the river consists of bored concrete piles with a pile cap supporting a circular concrete pier. This pivot pier houses the bearings, hydraulics and lifting equipment which support the bridge while turning. The abutments are of reinforced concrete founded on bored piles behind the quay walls. The piles for the support pier and both abutments were bored 20 metres down to the limestone rock under the river bed.

The asymmetric design, by Santiago Calatrava, reflects a harp laid on its side. The cable-stayed, steel pylon curves northwards to a point 48 metres above the river while its base is set outside the river's navigational channel and 28 metres from the south quay wall. The harp formation consists of 25 forestay cables of 60 mm diameter. The six backstay cables are of 145 mm diameter. When opening the vertical load of 5,850 tonnes is lifted 75 mm and two hydraulic cylinders rotate the bridge 90 degrees operating as a push-pull system. The superstructure was fabricated in one piece in Rotterdam in the Netherlands.

The bridge crosses the river at right angles, the deck consisting of pedestrian, cycle and traffic lanes in a configuration that can also accommodate trams. The bridge width varies from 28 to 33 metres.

Roughan and O'Donovan, Consulting Engineers, collaborated on the project while the bridge was built by Graham Hollandia Joint Venture Contractors. The cost was €60 million.

In 2010, the Samuel Beckett Bridge won the Engineers Ireland Award. A brass plaque commemorates the opening of the bridge on 10th December, 2009.

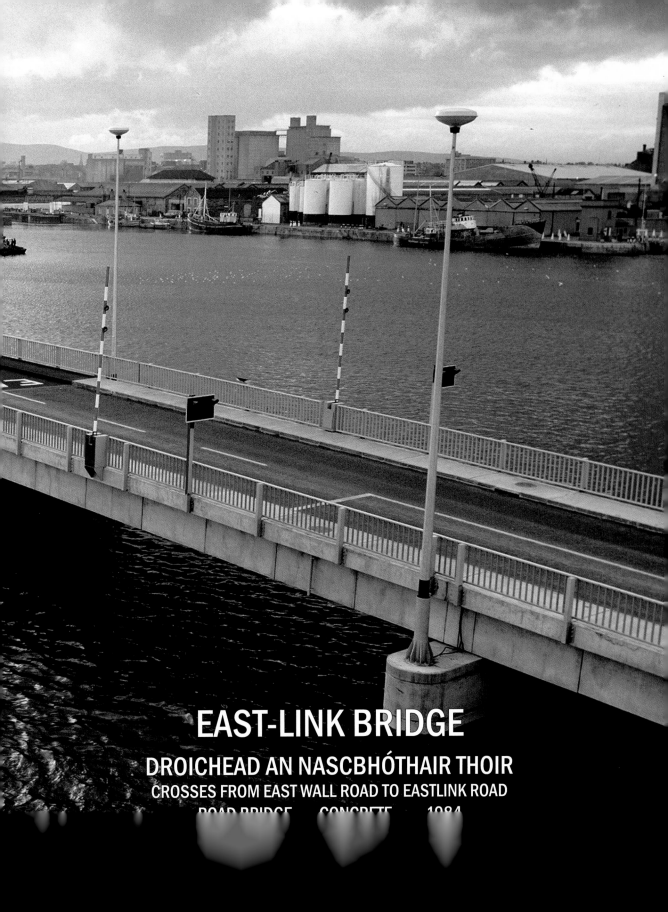

EAST-LINK BRIDGE

DROICHEAD AN NASCBHÓTHAIR THOIR

CROSSES FROM EAST WALL ROAD TO EASTLINK ROAD

ROAD BRIDGE   CONCRETE   1984

Left: an aerial view of the East-Link Bridge. The lifting span is open, allowing the newly-commissioned Naval Service 'LÉ Samuel Beckett' to sail upriver.

The most easterly of all the Liffey bridges, the East-Link spans the Liffey at its widest point, just as the bay begins. It crosses from East Wall Road on the north bank to Eastlink Road on the south.

In older times, Ringsend was a place apart, a peninsula separated from Dublin by the estuary of the River Dodder. It was a once lawless slobland remote from the Vikings in their upriver colony, their Norman successors and from the medieval city of Dublin that later emerged. In time, a settlement grew here, where deep water allowed ships to transfer goods to smaller boats for shipment upriver. Oliver Cromwell arrived at Ringsend in 1649. A ferry service is recorded as operating here across the Liffey as early as 1665.

In time, the area north and south of the river became the home of industry, usually that of the more dangerous and olfactory kind, such as fertilizer and vitriol factories. Tight-knit communities of big families, living in small terraced houses grew up on both the north and south sides. However, until the advent of this bridge in 1984, there was no fixed link nearby between these communities.

Captain Bligh (of 'Bounty' fame, a skilled navigator, and a competent surveyor) carried out a survey at the beginning of the 19th century. His proposal was for the building of a wall on the north side of the channel. This, when completed, along with the existing south wall, increased the flow of water to naturally sweep away the silt, and deepen the channel. Ships of deeper draught could now sail upriver. Dublin Port grew in the latter half of the 19th century, and new quays were built, in an inexorable move eastwards.

Fast-forward to the last quarter of the 20th century. Car ownership was on the rise and Dublin was beginning to experience severe traffic congestion. In 1976, the same year in which construction began on the Talbot Memorial Bridge, traffic studies highlighted the necessity for a further relief bridge downriver. However, desirable as the project was, public funds were scarce

Below: barrier down, red lights flashing. The bridge is open for river traffic.

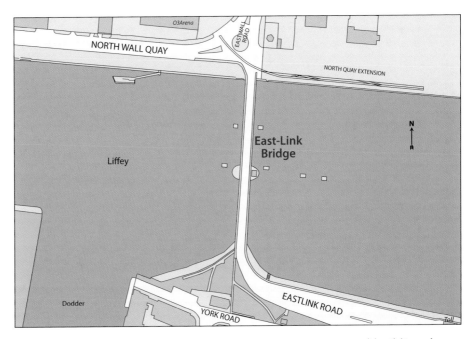

in those austere economic times. A private company proposed building the bridge and sought to operate it on a pay-to-use basis – this was to be Dublin's first modern toll bridge.

Exacting a toll from travellers is a custom as old as roads and bridges themselves. The 14th-century monks who operated Dublin's first stone bridge, St John's Bridge, did just that, bestowing holy water and a blessing in return. In the time of King George II, the Turnpike Act of 1731 allowed for the making of toll roads, with the tolls financing their construction and upkeep. With the coming of the railways their popularity decreased and the act was repealed in 1854. The last known such agreement in the city was for the construction of the pedestrian Ha'penny Bridge in 1816 – which itself replaced a ferry service – and the levy of a ha'penny for all users. That toll ceased in 1919.

A ground-breaking public-private partnership agreement was developed and in 1979 the Local Government (Toll Roads) Act paved the way for National Toll Roads to proceed with their proposed bridge.

Construction began in April 1983 to a design by McCarthy and Partners, Consulting Engineers (with Dorman Long Bridge and Engineering). Irishenco Ltd with Thompsons of Carlow were responsible for construction. In accordance with the contract agreement, throughout the project the river remained navigable.

The East-Link Bridge does not give an impression of any great architectural beauty. One might guess that it was designed with an emphasis on functionality, rather than aesthetics. It has four fixed concrete spans of 26 metres each and a 45 metre steel, opening span. This opening section can be raised and lowered using counterweights.

Sections of the opening span were fabricated in Carlow and transported to Alexandra Basin in the port. The separate units were aligned on support

trestles and welded in sequence. The completed opening span was then ferried out by a floating 400-tonne Sheerleg crane and placed directly into position, in an operation that took less than four hours.

The shipping channel, open when the lifting span is raised, is off centre, nearer the north bank. The single leaf opening span was chosen to pivot from the main central pier to give a more symmetrical appearance. This middle pier houses the lifting system of twin-cylindered hydraulics and also a deep shaft into which the counterweight rotates.

The bridge is supported on steel piles driven between 12 and 14 metres deep through black boulder clay to the Liffey bedrock. Unseen by bridge users, the movement of the opening span, weighing 500 tonnes, is controlled by a microprocessor which also synchronises the traffic, the warning lights and the road barriers.

The bridge is 10 metres wide with one traffic lane and footpath in each direction. As part of the project, it was also necessary to construct an approach road to the south, around a kilometre long, to connect with adjacent main roads.

Above: with the opening span at near vertical, the bridge changes from the functional to the dramatic.

Project management was rigorous, and conscious of time and money, took the same no-nonsense approach as the bridge design. The fixed-cost contract allowed for 80 weeks to completion. To a cacophonous fanfare of ships' horns the East-Link Bridge was declared open on 21st October 1984, week 81 of the project. Taoiseach Garrett Fitzgerald and the Lord Mayor of Dublin, Michael O'Halloran had the dual honour of pulling the lever that lowers the central opening span.

The bridge quickly proved of great benefit – traffic congestion in the wider area was reduced and it cut over three kilometres off some cross-city journeys. For the first time there was a direct road link between the local communities on the north and south shores. And for the last time, the local ferries across the river, for so long a familiar sight, crossed this stretch of water.

The East-Link may appear drab on a dreary winter's day, particularly in comparison to its stunning neighbour, the Samuel Beckett upriver. Yet, workaday bridge as it is, the East-Link has had its moments of glory and none more so than when the Tall Ships Festival, co-sponsored by Dublin City Council, came to town. Through this maritime gateway passes a splendid parade of impressive sailing ships. Commanding as it does the entrance to the city, the East-Link changes from the functional to the dramatic. When the alarm bell rings and the road barrier has descended, the giant steel span then lifts skywards making a dramatic opening statement: 'Welcome to Dublin!'

The Structure

The East-Link Bridge is a five-span, bascule-type bridge. It spans from East Wall Road on the north bank to Eastlink Road on the south.

The main pier, located at the southern end of the cantilever bascule, is a concrete box, supported on driven steel piles and constructed within a sheet-piled cofferdam. It contains a twin-cylindered hydraulic controlled lifting apparatus and a deep central shaft which accommodates the counterweight as it rotates.

The south abutment and wing walls were constructed within a sheet-pile cofferdam due to their levels. To preserve the existing masonry quay wall, the north abutment was located behind the quay wall. Both abutments were constructed on steel H-piles.

The four fixed approach spans of 26 metres each are precast, pre-stressed beams, with an in-situ concrete slab deck, which sit on reinforced concrete piers bearing on piles driven through the black boulder clay to the bedrock.

The single-leaf, steel opening span is 45 metres long and lifts through 80 degrees in under one minute. The bridge width is 10 metres.

The bridge was designed by McCarthy and Partners, Consultant Engineers with Dorman Long Bridge and Engineering. Irishenco Ltd with Thompsons of Carlow were responsible for construction. It opened on 21st October 1984 and the cost was £6.1 million.

Chapter 4

THE CITY, ITS RIVER AND BRIDGES
AN CHATHAIR, A hABHAINN AGUS A DROICHID

A bridge, the Liffey and the Four Courts, seen in 1850

The story of Dublin's bridges is intertwined with the history of the city and the Liffey. When the Vikings arrived well over a millennium ago there was a ford across the river which, in time, they replaced with a simple timber structure. Bridges of increasing sophistication were steadily built during the different eras: that of the Normans; the time of expansion by the Duke of Ormonde and the sprint for growth in the Georgian era when Dublin became the second city of the empire. More bridges were built during the 19th and 20th centuries. As Dublin continues to grow, new bridges are still being built, attuned to present needs. Throughout time the Liffey bridges of Dublin have not been merely passages across a great river, but architectural gems, keepers of history and destinations of note.

'Riverrun, past Eve and Adam's, from swerve of shore to bend of bay'.
'Finnegans Wake', by James Joyce

The River Liffey, Dublin Bay and the city together form a splendid trinity. Hewn by nature and wrought by man through a thousand years and more of turbulent history it is, as ever was, the river – the spring water and sea foam of Anna Livia – which nourishes this trinity's existence. For it was the river which drew the first settlers, who sailed into the bay. Its water provided nourishment, fertile shores as well as communication with their faraway homeland.

Who named this ancient river? The Liffey, Abhainn Life, Avenlif and Joyce's Anna Livia Plurabelle – all these names most likely derive from *Magh Life,* the rich plain or *Magh* of County Kildare through which the Liffey loops and curls on her way to the sea. In ancient Ireland the *Magh* was also an order of priests. The Liffey, a mere bog stream born in the Wicklow mountains, magically swells, grows and teems with life as it gathers pace through the plain, blessing the populace with abundant food.

Whatever its origins, it is a powerful name, adopted by Cairbre Liffeachair, 3rd-century monarch of Ireland who married the daughter of the legendary Fionn MacCumhaill. It is a name which slipped off the tongues of people through history, from the time of the Vikings down to present times. Over the centuries, the Liffey has been altered and moulded in every era.

Arrival of the Vikings
The first Viking longboat, the oars of 50 men slicing through the water in unison and sailing high on the waves of the Irish Sea, rounded into Dublin Bay and sailed up the river more than 1,200 years ago. The Norsemen's intent was not peaceful – they had brought marauding and piracy to a new level. They invaded, they battled, they won and enjoyed the spoils. Sometimes, enticed by the promise of a special place, they stayed.

So, from the moment these first Norsemen ascended a hill and triumphantly erected their trademark pillar stone on the south bank of the river, opposite where Gandon's Custom House stands today, the story of the Liffey changed. The primeval scene of meadow, marshes and meandering river was changed as more Norsemen arrived and settled. The warlike figureheads of their longboats crowded the river mouth and the air grew thick with the rancid smell of the horse fat used to grease the sails.

The rising tide brought them upriver to a great tidal bay – below where Christ Church stands today – cradled by gentle hills which swept from behind, forming a protective bluff on the seaward side and encircled by the dark river Poddle which pooled fresh water near its meeting with the Liffey. The Vikings felled trees and built houses of wattle and mud. The new Viking settlement became their principal base. From here, they staged daring raids as far south as the Mediterranean. On return, they carried their booty up from the Liffey shallows on high tide and into their shoreside settlement.

Below: replica of a Viking warship originally built in the Viking settlement of Dublin, on display at the National Museum of Ireland, Collins Barracks.

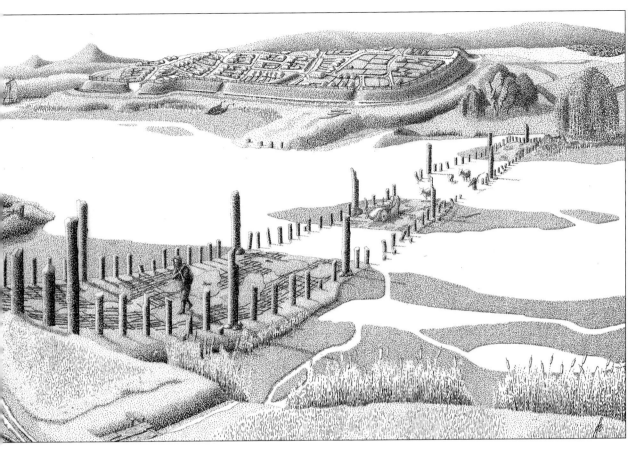

Geography of a River

More than 500 metres above sea level, deep in the Wicklow wilderness and a mere 20 km or so south of Dublin, the River Liffey rises in the mountains, running through soft mountain bog. From this splendid isolation it begins a long, meandering journey, coursing west, north and northeast, through Wicklow and Kildare, before making its final, eastward turn towards Dublin, completing a 125 km-long odyssey.

The Vikings' riverscape began where the Liffey's journey ended and a mere axe throw away they claimed land, near where Wood Quay stands today, and made their homes. What was the riverside like then? It was a wide river mouth around where is now the most easterly of the Liffey bridges – the East-Link. As the longboats sailed in from the bay, the river narrowed into a channel around where the Talbot Memorial Bridge stands. Along the top of where Townsend Street is today, there was rising land, later to be known as Lazar's Hill. Taking a south westerly turn, past jutting promontories, they sailed past another southside bay, where Gandon would, centuries later, build a great bridge, later rebuilt as O'Connell Bridge. Bays, loughs, rivers and streams, many forgotten and some later to be named – Poddle, Cadslough, the Pill, Bradogue – opened out before them to the north and south. They navigated a great reef – in time named Standfast Dick – barring the river channel west of where the Ha'penny Bridge now stands.

They chose for their settlement an escarpment which curved around a tidal bay and upon which, a few centuries later, Christ Church Cathedral was built. Nearby pooled the waters of the River Poddle – the *Dubh Linn* or Black Pool – and a river crossing, the ford of *Áth Cliath*, built by the native Irish. As the river curved west there were more loughs, streams, valleys and fertile hinterlands all the way to the end of the tidal reach at a place later known as Chapelizod. The Vikings set about moulding the riverscape in the area roughly around present-day Temple Bar. They piled earth into a bank, holding back the river with wooden posts – creating a 'wood quay' which changed the ancient riverscape. They also built a simple wooden bridge.

Above: at the Chapel Royal in Dublin Castle, the Irish king, Brian Boru manifest in stone.

The Coming of the Normans

The Normans came to Dublin, not by sailing up the Liffey, but by land, marching from the south. They invaded by invitation – an overture by Dermot McMurrough, exiled King of Leinster. McMurrough hoped to win back his kingdom, lost in a dispute with the High King of Ireland. He inveigled Richard de Clare, the legendary Strongbow, to help him regain power.

Dublin fell to the Normans in 1170 and the Viking settlers fled to the north bank of the Liffey to settle at Oxmanstown. Strongbow, by now married to Dermot's daughter Aoife, exerted firm control. The Norman King Henry II made a visit in 1172, to curb Strongbow's power. In 1177, Henry declared his son John, Lord of Ireland. John unexpectedly inherited the kingship and thus the lordship of Ireland was tied to the English throne.

And what did all this mean for Dublin and the Liffey? The Normans possessed superior technology, knowledge and administrative know-how which they put to good use in times of war – and peace. The city walls were strengthened and a stone castle was erected. A charter, allowing the city its first stone bridge, was granted to the city by King John in 1215. The river became even busier, with ships anchored two and three deep along the shore line. The area now known as Merchant's Quay developed and Wood Quay too was a focus of much river activity.

The population rapidly grew from around 1,000 at the time of invasion to one of several thousands more. A growing population required services and the Normans turned their innate inventiveness to providing Dublin with its first piped water supply.

Water, the Essence of Life

The ruling Normans, having dismissed the Vikings to the seclusion of the river's north banks set about laying water pipes as early as 1244 with a supply running from the Poddle to their new castle on the hill by 1245.

Across the Liffey, set in rich meadowland – where, today, the Four Courts stands – was the priory of St Saviour's. The Dominican friars, an institutionally powerful force, demanded piped water too.

Perhaps they were, belatedly, spurred into action by their brothers in religion, the monks of Kilmainham, who, in 1210, had dammed the Liffey, by

Above: again at the Chapel Royal, St Patrick, who brought Christianity to Ireland.

present-day Islandbridge. There may even have been a certain rivalry between the two over fishing rights on the river – a large net fixed by the old bridge was forcibly removed by the monks of Kilmainham, as it interfered with their fishing.

The Kilmainham weir ensured a fresh water supply for the monks and altered the natural order – the Liffey was no longer tidal as far as Chapelizod. The monks of St Saviour's, in turn, got their fresh water supply through a feat of medieval engineering. Water was piped from the Poddle to a large tank overlooking the river. From here pipes were laid across the new stone bridge – where Father Mathew's Bridge stands today – and from around the year 1308, the monks could enjoy their new water supply, albeit a mere trickle from a pipe no wider than a finger.

There followed four hundred long years. The town grew and overflowed into unruly suburbs, which spread outside the walls. The old bridge straddling the Liffey grew heavy with shops and houses. The river itself was the receptacle for all of the city's excesses – from domestic chamber pots, slaughterhouses, markets and bloody murder.

The Age of Expansion

The city was to change when James Butler, Duke of Ormonde, first arrived in Dublin as Viceroy (or Lord Lieutenant) of Ireland in 1662. He energetically set about improving everything – the streetscape, riverscape and water supply.

He put the River Liffey at the heart of the city by directing the expansion of the city onto the north bank of the Liffey – aided by developers, some more greedy than scrupulous. Bridges were vital to this plan, though Ormonde had to face down the resistance of ferry owners who saw their livelihoods threatened. Obviously he was not a man to be trifled with as within 14 years four new bridges graced the Liffey – the architectural ancestors of Grattan, O'Donovan Rossa, Mellows and Rory O'More Bridges. The pace of development was such that, a mere 100 years after Ormonde first assumed office, Dublin's Viking riverscape had all but disappeared. With bridges came the first series of long quay walls. The Liffey was contained along the length of the city, interspersed here and there with shingle strands and old houses and warehouses overhanging the water. Mudflats were still exposed at low tides beyond the Bloody Bridge. Sailing boats anchored three-deep at the (then) Custom House, located just downriver of Essex Bridge.

In 1670 a larger reservoir increased the city's water supply and the Old Bridge, dating from early Norman times, was once again called into service, carrying a water main to supplement the north side's supply from the River Bradogue, which trickled down from Cabra. Ormonde's reach went beyond the city limits. He commissioned a new bridge to cross the Liffey at Chapelizod, near the site of his out-of-town residence which became known as the King's House.

Left: the Chapel Royal of Dublin Castle is a good location to see the array of names of the Viceroys of Ireland. The Duke of Richmond's shield is to the immediate left of the organ. Many of the Viceroys (Richmond, Ormonde and others) had Dublin bridges named after them. None of these names survived in the extensive renaming exercise that took place after Independence.

A PROSPECT of the CITY

A MAP of the CITY and Suburbs of DUBLIN And alfo the ARCH BISHOP and EAR

Mapping Dublin and the River Liffey

Nearly 2,000 years ago, Ptolemy, a Graeco-Egyptian cartographer, produced maps of the Roman Empire with the inhabited world on its edges. Ireland was included in a rudimentary map. He depicted a settlement called Eblana, which may or may not have been Dublin.

When John Speed, an English cartographer, published his map of Dublin in 1610 (see page 5), the Liffey, lovingly drawn, took pride of place – flowing by the walls of the old city which nestled on the south bank. East and west of the walls, bays, inlets and strands shape the riverscape while, opposite, the north bank, little inhabited, has creeks and marshland between the walls of the religious house, St Mary's, and the Inns. The Liffey is busy with trading vessels, some anchored at 'The Bridge', which boasts a defensive gateway, controlling access to the city. Quaintly, Speed measures Dublin – which stretches from the 'Colledge' to the remote St. James' Gate – in 'paces', with Merchant's and Wood 'Keys' running together for a length of around 400 of these.

Bernard de Gomme, a Dutchman, surveyed Dublin, publishing his plan in 1673. Already the Duke of Ormonde had made his mark: two bridges now straddled 'The Liffy'. Where Westmoreland and D'Olier Streets are today, the ground is marked as 'taken in from the sea' and protected by a wall, rendering Trinity College safe from tidal floods and marking the Temple Bar area on a map for the first time. William Usher's Island is named beyond the Old Bridge, opposite which the suburbs north of the river are taking rudimentary shape. The 'City of Dublin' is still contained within the old walls and Merchant's and Wood Keys now run into Back Key. The River Poddle has been culverted and its bay filled in. Out on the north-eastern shores of the Liffey – where Rosie Hackett Bridge is today – is a remote outpost of six houses. A

Above: Charles Brooking's 1728 panorama 'A Prospect of the City of Dublin from the North'. Contrast this with the further growth and development shown in the panoramic view published in the 'Illustrated London News' of 1849, looking from the south, as shown in the endpapers of this book.

of DUBLIN from the NORTH.

1 Rings End	11 S.t Michaels
2 The new Library	12 S.t Lukes
3 The College	13 S.t John's in
4 The Round Chur	Thomas Street
5 The Castle	14 S.t Catherines
6 The Theatell	15 S.t James's
7 S.t Patricks Ch:	16 The Poor House
8 S.t Warburohs	17 The Royal Hospl
9 Christ Church	18 S.t Georges
10 S.t Johns	19 The Glass house

MEATHS Liberties with the bounds of each PARISH. Drawn from an Actual SURVEY. Made by Charles Brooking

1714 map of Dublin, beautifully blocked and coloured by cartographer Herman Moll, shows the Liffey's complement of new bridges. Beyond the most easterly, Essex Bridge (Grattan Bridge), and to the sea, was muddy strand, laid bare at low tide. Charles Brooking's 1728 panorama 'A Prospect of the City of Dublin from the North' sweeps across the cluttered rooflines of the city from the stately Royal Hospital at Kilmainham out to the bay, where the Liffey is now contained by the north, east and south walls in various stages of completion. His map of the same date reveals that de Gomme's six lone houses have been encompassed into a gentle urban sprawl. Neele's late 18th-century map depicts Greater Dublin ringed by circular roads to the north and south, and bursting with vibrant business, commercial and social life. Importantly for the development of the Liffey and its bridges, control of Dublin Port was ceded from Dublin Corporation to the Ballast Board, newly established in 1776. All told, the 18th century had been a time of great splendour for Dublin – its Georgian period of glory.

Overleaf: 'A View of Dublin from the Park'. This 18th-century print captures the essence of Dublin – in the foreground, the Liffey and Island Bridge are framed by two great initiatives of the Duke of Ormonde – Phoenix Park and the Royal Hospital. In the background is the expanding city.

The Act of Union of 1801

However, all was to change. The political and titled classes abandoned Dublin when on 1st January 1801 the Act of Union joined Ireland, England and Scotland into the United Kingdom. Parliament House, a stone's throw from the Liffey, fell quiet. Dublin did not grow much during the 19th century. From once being the second city of the British Empire, it fell, by 1900, to being the tenth. Strangely, as if trying to keep the life blood flowing through the city, the Liffey riverscape underwent a period of regeneration even as the genteel squares of Georgian Dublin descended into tenements. Five new bridges – the Ha'penny and the Richmond (O'Donovan Rossa) Bridges in 1816, the Whitworth (Father Mathew) Bridge in 1818, the King's (Sean Heus-

227

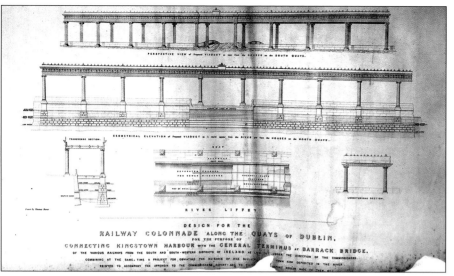

DESIGN FOR THE
RAILWAY COLONNADE ALONG THE QUAYS OF DUBLIN,
FOR THE PURPOSE OF
CONNECTING KINGSTOWN HARBOUR WITH THE GENERAL TERMINUS AT BARRACK BRIDGE,

The bridges over the Liffey that never were — there were many schemes for bridges that never materialised.

Left: in 1834, pioneering railway engineer, Charles Blacker Vignoles, prepared a proposal for an elevated railway viaduct to run along the Liffey quays to connect the Dublin & Kingstown Railway (of which he was engineer during its construction) with the west.

COMPETITION DESIGNS FOR NEW CARLISLE BRIDGE.

MESSRS. TURNER AND PAGE.— FIRST PRIZE.

Left: the winning design by George Page and Richard Turner for a replacement of Carlisle Bridge. (Turner was the great Ballsbridge ironfounder who made the palmhouses at Kew and Glasnevin.) In the event this design was not used; rather the actual design for what is today's O'Connell Bridge (1880) was by the innovative Victorian engineer, Bindon Blood Stoney.

Left: artist's impression of the modern art gallery (proposed by Hugh Lane to house his collection) located on a new bridge over the river, which was to have replaced the Ha'penny Bridge. The design, by the architect Sir Edwin Lutyens was adopted by Dublin Corporation in 1913. Luckily, it never proceeded.

230

Above: Dublin's bridges have forever been busy, none more so than the widest of them all. Here is the scene from Carlisle Bridge of the celebration in 1875 of the centenary O'Connell's birth. In 1880 it was reconstructed and was renamed O'Connell Bridge.

ton) Bridge in 1828 and in the far-flung suburb of Lucan the new bridge of 1813 – were built. The quays too were improved by the Ballast Board. From an uneven collection of quaysides there emerged, by 1830, the modern quayscape, the Liffey framed by uniform granite walls topped with attractive copings. As the port expanded in the age of the steamship, quay extensions were completed downriver. The growing importance of the river and port was acknowledged when the influential Dublin Port and Docks Board replaced the Ballast Board.

Seven bridges were completed or rebuilt in the second part of the 19th century, including the majestic O'Connell Bridge in 1880 and the industrial-looking Loop Line Bridge. And then there was the stink. In the mid-1800s, from Barrack (Rory O'More) Bridge to Carlisle (O'Connell) Bridge – 181 sewers emptied their untreated contents into a two kilometre stretch of river. As the 19th century progressed there was greater understanding of the link between air and water-borne disease and the need for a proper means of sewage disposal. Experts in the newly developing field of public health began to develop plans for comprehensive sewage systems. Work on a city sewage system for Dublin finally commenced in 1896 and it was in operation by 1906. Buried beneath the quays are giant interceptor sewers which direct all waste to the Ringsend pumping station. The city could breathe again – almost. The foul-smelling Camac still emptied directly into the river until around 1980.

Independence

As the 20th century dawned, the momentum for Irish independence began to accelerate. Dublin was where most of the significant events occured. In 1913, during the Lockout, families queued for food rations at Liberty Hall, by the Loop Line Bridge. It was from Liberty Hall that the Volunteers strode out on their way to the GPO on Easter Monday in 1916. By the middle of Easter week the gunship *Helga* sailed up the Liffey and shelled Liberty Hall, aiming under the spans of the Loop Line Bridge.

Deadly conflict was to play out across the city twice more – first during the War of Independence (1919-21) and then during the Civil War (1922-23). Flames flared up by the Liffey on many occasions: when Sackville (O'Connell) Street burned in 1916; the burning of the Custom House in 1921 and the shelling and explosion at the Four Courts in 1922. As Ireland settled into nationhood and Dublin rebuilt her architectural treasures, the innate beauty of the Liffey and her bridges was often overlooked in favour of more functional schemes. There were many: a 1913 scheme to replace the Ha'penny Bridge with a 'highway' over the Liffey from Henry Street to Dame Street; in the 1920s Dublin Corporation investigated the possibility of replacing the Loop Line Bridge with a railway tunnel under the Liffey. In 1929 a 'Transporter Bridge' which would swing cars and citizens across the river on a gondola, just where the Samuel Beckett Bridge is today, was proposed and legislated for. In the event, only the new Butt Bridge of 1932 went ahead, as the old bridge was too narrow and steep to cater for growing city traffic.

A 1924 agreement between Dublin Corporation, the Dublin Port and Docks Board and Pembroke UDC for a pedestrian tunnel under the Liffey was reduced to a service tunnel on the grounds of cost. It was duly bored from near East Wall Road to Thorncastle Street in Ringsend. Advice from the City Engineer and the Planning Officer was sought in 1960 on a proposal to cover over the Liffey in whole or in part to provide car parking facilities. One scheme envisaged an extended bridge spanning the river at lengths and the other a shelf-type structure extending out from the quays, between bridges, and covering half the river width. The plan failed due to difficulties of construction, flooding concerns and the general unsightliness.

Had the 1973 Central Dublin Traffic Plan been approved today's Liffey-scape would be much busier, totally in thrall to the car. The plan offered a number of options, all including a motorway bridge to be built in approximately the same location as the East-Link Bridge. Near the centre city and its old bridges a trinity of concrete bridges was proposed. One would fly high over the Liffey, accompanied at quay level by two further bridges. This scheme faded into deserved obscurity. The ever-increasing problem of city traffic, and the growing business of the port (since 1997 the responsibility of the Dublin Port Company), was less obtrusively dealt with by the construction of two road bridges to the east, the Talbot Memorial in 1978 and the East-Link in 1984, one westerly city bridge, the Frank Sherwin in 1982 and the West-Link Bridge of 1990, itself part of the orbital M50 motorway.

Dublin bridges featured during the turmoil of the early 20th-century.

Right: an improvised armoured car races by O'Connell Bridge, in the last days of Easter Week, during the 1916 Rising. Lower Sackville (O'Connell) Street, is in ruins, ravaged by fire and shells.

On Wednesday morning, 26th April 1916, the armed yacht 'Helga' sailed upriver, and despite the intervening bridge, fired 24 rounds at Liberty Hall, which was also shelled by a British 18-pounder at Tara Street. Near right: headquarters of the ITGWU, Liberty Hall in ruins, in the shadow of the Loop Line Bridge.

Far right: 'HMY Helga'.

Below near right: with Mellows Bridge in the foreground, the Four Courts explodes on 30th June 1922, at the start of the Irish Civil War.

Far right: crowds assemble in early July 1922, to look along O'Connell Bridge towards Sackville Street, newly in ruins after the fighting between the anti- and pro-Treaty forces.

Overleaf: three bridges swing open to allow access upriver, September 2015. River and sea traffic, including liners, can sail as far as the Talbot Memorial Bridge.

AFTER THE BOMBARDMENT
The Holocaust of Ireland's Greatest Thoroughfare
EASTER WEEK 1916.
From the Painting by A. McGOOGAN
Now in possession of the New Ireland Assurance Co. Ltd. Dublin

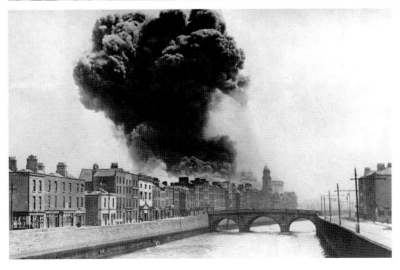

233

Today's Liffey

As 1999 turned to 2000, the renaissance of the Dublin docklands had begun in earnest, possibly the most startling change of the lands by the Liffey since James Butler, Duke of Ormonde expanded the city on the river's north banks in the late 1600s. On the run-down quays east of the city, glass and steel monuments to Mammon rose, as the new financial centre was developed. Dublin began to enjoy a period of economic growth – it was time to start building bridges again. With ever-increasing traffic on the M50, the West-Link Bridge was doubled in 2002.

In time, there was a realisation that the rise of car traffic could not continue unabated. Within the city itself, pedestrian- and environmentally-friendly transport options became the focus, and bridges were planned and provided in support of this. The Ha'penny Bridge, exclusively for pedestrians, was restored and reopened in December 2001. Santiago Calatrava's first collaboration with the city of Dublin, the James Joyce Bridge, opened on Bloomsday, 16th June 2003, accommodating vehicular traffic but with special consideration for the pedestrian and places to sit for the weary. The Seán O'Casey Bridge of 2005 is for pedestrians only and crucially facilitates all river traffic, including liners, accessing upstream as far as the Talbot Memorial Bridge. The Rosie Hackett Bridge accommodates both pedestrians and public transport. The Samuel Beckett was opened in December 2009. The acclaimed Calatrava design marks the renaissance of the eastern docklands and is an impressive sight approaching the city from the bay. It is a statement of confidence in a city, its river and its people. It is a jewel in the city's collection of bridges, ancient and modern. If you travel to see them, salute each bridge as you cross for they are not merely passages across a great river, but architectural gems, essential markers of the history of the city and destinations of note – the Bridges of Dublin.

Above: the most elegant and beautiful of the Liffey bridges? The Samuel Beckett Bridge is a strong contender for this accolade in the continuing story of Dublin's bridges, spanning the river, one thousand years on.

BIBLIOGRAPHY

Papers

Bond, E.W., *Reconstruction of Butt Bridge, Dublin,* IEI Transactions, Vol 59, 1932

Mallagh, J., *City Bridges over the Liffey, present and future,* IEI Transactions, Vol 65, 1939

Phillips M., Hamilton A., *Project History of Dublin's River Liffey Bridges,* Proc. ICE, London, BE 156, 2003

Stephens L.F., Dowling M.E., *Talbot Memorial Bridge Dublin,* IEI Transactions, Vol 102, 1978

Publications

Barry, Michael, *Across Deep Waters, Bridges of Ireland,* Frankfort Press, 1985

Barry, Michael, *Courage Boys, We are Winning, an Illustrated History of the 1916 Rising,* Andalus Press, 2015

Barry, Michael, *The Green Divide, an Illustrated History of the Irish Civil War,* Andalus Press, 2014

Barry, Michael, *Victorian Dublin Revealed,* Andalus Press, 2011

Beckett, J. C., *The Making of Modern Ireland 1603-1923,* faber and faber, 1972

Bennet, Douglas, *The Encyclopedia of Dublin,* Gill & Macmillan, 2005

Bolger, Muriel, *Dublin, City of Literature,* O'Brien Press, 2011

Bradshaw, George, *Bradshaw's Handbook for Tourists in Great Britain and Ireland,* Nabu Press, 2012

Brewer, J. N., *The Beauties of Ireland,* Ulan Press, 2012

Casey, Christine, *The Buildings of Ireland: Dublin,* Yale University Press, 2005

Collins, James, *Life in Old Dublin,* Forgotten Books, 2015

Connolly, S., ed., *The Oxford Companion to Irish History,* Oxford University Press, 1998

Corcoran, Michael, *Our Good Health, a History of Dublin's Water and Drainage,* Four Courts Press, 2006

Cox, Ronald, *Bindon Blood Stoney,* IEI, 1990

Cox, Ronald; Donald, Philip, *Ireland's Civil Engineering Heritage,* Collins Press, 2013

Cox, Ronald; Gould, Michael, *Ireland's Bridges,* Wolfhound Press, 2003

De Courcy, John, *The Liffey in Dublin,* Gill and Macmillan, 1996

Doyle, Oliver; Hirsch, Stephen, *Railways in Ireland 1834-1984,* Signal Press, 1983

Ferrar, John , *A View of Ancient and Modern Dublin, with its improvements to the year 1796,* Forgotten Books, 2015

Fitzpatrick, Samuel, *Dublin: A Historical and Topographical Account of the City,* Ulan Press, 2012

Gandon, James, *The Life of James Gandon,* Nabu Press, 2010

Gilbert, John Thomas, *Calendar of Ancient Records of Dublin in the Possession of the Municipal Corporation of that City,* Ulan Press, 2012

Gilbert, John Thomas, *A History of the City of Dublin,* Forgotten Books, 2012

Holinshed, Raphael, *Chronicles of England, Scotland and Ireland,* 2012

Johnson, Stephen, *Johnson's Atlas and Gazetteer of the Railways of Ireland,* Midland Publishing, 1997

Joyce, Weston St John, *The Neighbourhood of Dublin,* Skellig, 1988

Lee, Joseph, *The Modernisation of Irish Society 1848-1918,* Gill and Macmillan, 1992

McCullough, Niall, *Dublin, an Urban History,* Anne Street Press, 1989

O'Donnell, E.E., *The Annals of Dublin: Fair City,* Merlin Publishing, 1987

O'Keefe, Peter, *Irish Stone Bridges,* Irish Academic Press, 1991

Peter, Ada, *Sketches of Old Dublin,* Forgotten Books, 2015

Plowden, Francis, *The History of Ireland: from Its Invasion Under Henry II to Its Union with Britain,* Forgotten Books, 2015

Plunkett, James, *Strumpet City,* Hutchinson, 1969

Ruddock, Ted, *Arch Bridges and their Builders 1735-1835,* Cambridge University Press, 1998

Ryan, Christopher, *Lewis' Dublin,* Collins Press, 2001

Rynne, Colin, *Industrial Ireland 1750-1930,* Collins Press, 2006

Semple, George, *A Treatise on Building in Water in Two Parts,* Gale ECCO, Print Editions, 2010

Somerville Large, Peter, *Dublin,* Granada, 1979

Tutty, M.J., *Bridges over the Liffey,* Dublin Historical Record, Vol XXXV, 1981

ALONG THE LIFFEY

A Bridges Tour – to the West

Take a pleasant walk upriver. Go west on the boardwalk on the north river bank along Bachelors Walk to the most photographed structure in Dublin – the cast-iron **Ha'penny Bridge** (p 138), with its high arch over the river. It was constructed in 1816, manufactured of cast iron in Coalbrookdale in England. At first there was a pedestrian toll, requiring a ha'penny (hence the name) to cross.

The Ha'penny Bridge, at the heart of Dublin

Continue west along the boardwalk by the **Millennium Bridge** (p 130), a footbridge opened in 1999. Next is **Grattan Bridge** (p 120, at the intersection with Capel St), The delightful cast-iron lamp stands, decorated with seahorses, date from the reconstruction of 1875, sitting on the foundations of the previous Essex Bridge.

Continue west along the south quays, and we next encounter, in sequence, three masonry bridges from the Georgian era. Graceful and mainly constructed of granite, these are very much in harmony with the riverine setting, and complement the 18th-century Four Courts. First is **O'Donovan Rossa Bridge** (p 110), adjacent to Wood Quay. Note the keystone figures at the top of the elliptical arches. Next is the elliptical-arch **Father Mathew Bridge** (p 102), adjacent to Merchant's Quay, with cast-iron balusters. Continue and passing the Four Courts on the opposite bank, next is **Mellows Bridge** (p 94), adjacent to Usher's Quay. This is the oldest bridge in Dublin (1768), which is why the arches are of the simpler semi-circular shape.

Carved heads over the arches of O'Donovan Rossa Bridge

Next are the white futuristic lines of the **James Joyce Bridge** (p 84), adjacent to Usher's Quay. Here is the geometric style of the Spanish engineer and architect, Santiago Calatrava. The bridge is adjacent to 15 Usher's Quay, fictional scene of Joyce's best short story, *The Dead*. Continue westwards and we come next to the blue-painted cast-iron bridge, now called after **Rory O'More** (p 76) and opened in 1861. It was previously called the Victoria and Albert Bridge. Pass by Collins Barracks (the museum there is worth a detour).

Cast-iron elegance: Rory O'More Bridge

After the functional **Frank Sherwin Bridge** (p 68), we come to the **Seán Heuston Bridge**, (p 58) one of the finest over the river, now carrying *Luas* trams. To the left is Heuston (formerly Kingsbridge) railway station. Built in 1828, the arched bridge is a fine example of cast iron which was cast in a nearby ironworks. The corners of the bridge have crowns with the emblems of England, Wales, Scotland and Ireland. Note the sloping Egyptian-style granite abutments, a style that was popular in the 19th century. Like other Liffey bridges it has been renamed. There is irony in the change of name, from the original in honour of George IV, to that of Seán Heuston, one of the leaders of the 1916 Rising.

Calatrava's James Joyce Bridge

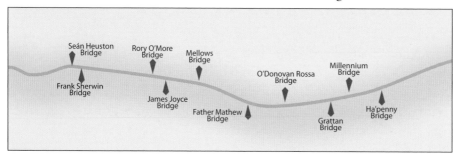

The cast-iron Seán Heuston Bridge

A Bridges Tour – to the East

Magisterial and wide: the O'Connell Bridge

New bridge on the block — the Rosie Hackett

Looking across the Seán O'Casey Bridge

The Liffey viewed from the locks at Grand Canal Dock.

Iconic – Calatrava's Samuel Beckett Bridge

Walk downriver, along the revitalised docklands quarter, to the mouth of the Liffey, to experience the shock of the new and some of the charm of the old.

Start from **O'Connell Bridge** (p 148) and walk east along the south quays. The original bridge of 1794 that connected O'Connell (then Sackville) Street was designed by Gandon. The present one was rebuilt in 1880. It was then the world's widest city bridge. It was named after the nationalist leader, Daniel O'Connell, whose large monument it faces.

First along is Dublin's newest bridge, the **Rosie Hackett**, (p 162) opened in 2014, dedicated solely to pedestrians and public transport. The 1960s Liberty Hall towers above the concete **Butt Bridge** (p 170) and the railway **Loop Line Bridge** (p 178) – which obscures a view of Dublin's finest building, Gandon's Custom House. Next is the concrete **Talbot Memorial Bridge** (p 190) and the IFSC buildings begin. Pass the pedestrian-only **Seán O'Casey Bridge**, (p 196) of attractive modern design.

At Sir John Rogerson's Quay, just past the Samuel Beckett Bridge, it is worth taking a detour – turn right up Cardiff Lane. You come to the Bord Gáis Energy Theatre. Turn left and you enter the new development around Grand Canal Dock. The dock here was once a thriving hub in the early 19th century, full of barges and small ships, from the time when the canal was the only way to move heavy goods inland. This was the terminus of the Grand Canal, completed in 1796, still navigable to much of the south and west of Ireland.

Continue east down the quay and at the end you see the three locks where the canal boats can descend from the higher dock and canal level down to the Liffey waters. You can see the names of long-forgotten Lords Lieutenant, Camden, Buckingham, and Westmoreland, carved on the stone walls.

Now retrace your steps to the **Samuel Beckett Bridge** (p 204). This opened in 2009 and is worth travelling to see. It is a particularly successful work by the Spanish engineer, Santiago Calatrava: its shape evokes a harp, symbol of Ireland. The white, soaring, Aeolian lines of the bridge fit in with the environment of modern buildings to be found all over the docklands. The bridge swings to allow vessels upriver.

Adjacent to the bridge is the Convention Centre with its glass atrium at the front, in the 'tilted can' style. Continue eastwards and you see a former light-ship, painted red, moored in front of the 3Arena, once a Victorian railway freight depot. From the footpath of the utilitarian **East-Link Bridge** (p 214) you have a good view downriver of the busy docks of Dublin Port, with the bay beyond.

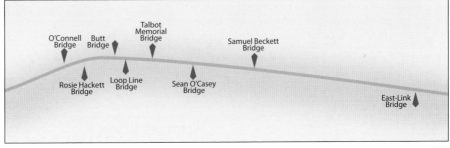

DRAWINGS OF BRIDGES

Presented here is a collection of drawings of the bridges over the Liffey, from Lucan to the sea. These drawings come from several sources, of differing quality and from different eras (not to scale).

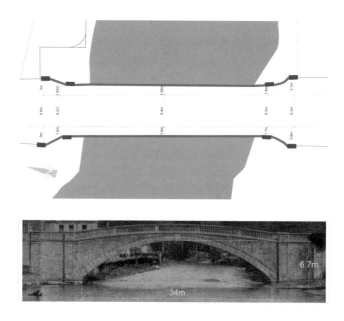

Lucan Bridge

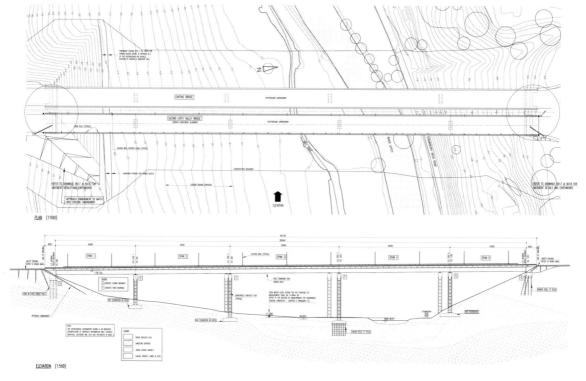

West-Link Bridge

Plan at deck level

Plan at top bracing level

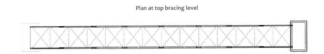

Long Section

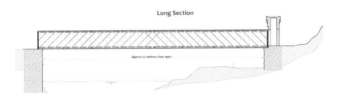

Approx 52 metres clear span

Farmleigh Bridge

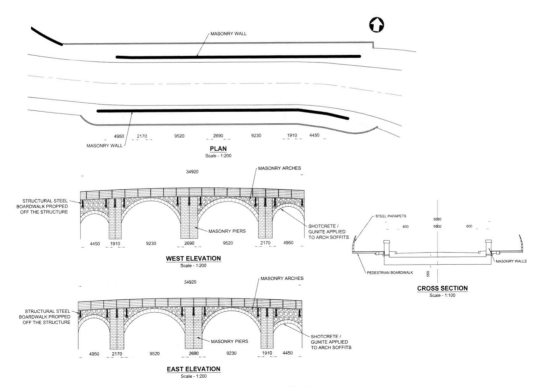

MASONRY WALL

4950 2170 9520 2690 9230 1910 4450

MASONRY WALL

PLAN
Scale - 1:200

34920

MASONRY ARCHES

STRUCTURAL STEEL
BOARDWALK PROPPED
OFF THE STRUCTURE

MASONRY PIERS

SHOTCRETE /
GUNITE APPLIED
TO ARCH SOFFITS

4450 1910 9230 2690 9520 2170 4950

WEST ELEVATION
Scale - 1:200

STEEL PARAPETS

8980
6500
600 600

PEDESTRIAN BOARDWALK

MASONRY WALLS

550

CROSS SECTION
Scale - 1:100

34920

MASONRY ARCHES

STRUCTURAL STEEL
BOARDWALK PROPPED
OFF THE STRUCTURE

MASONRY PIERS

SHOTCRETE /
GUNITE APPLIED
TO ARCH SOFFITS

4950 2170 9520 2690 9230 1910 4450

EAST ELEVATION
Scale - 1:200

Anna Livia Bridge

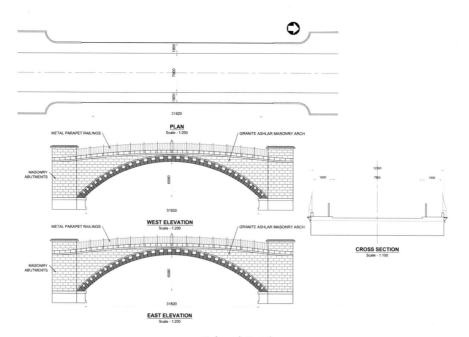

Island Bridge

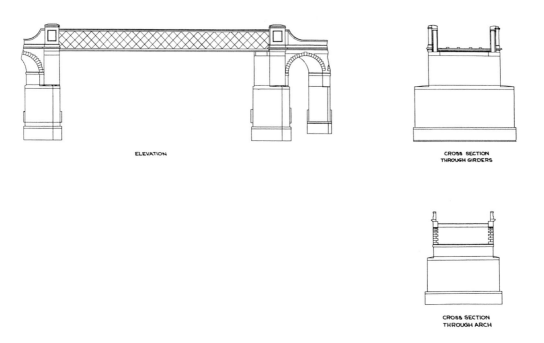

Liffey Railway Bridge

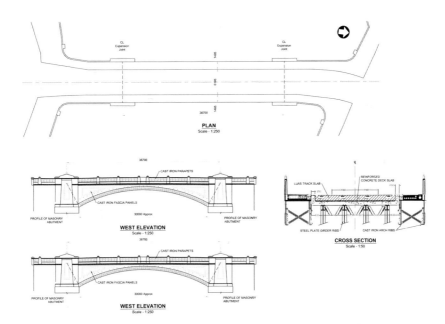

Seán Heuston Bridge

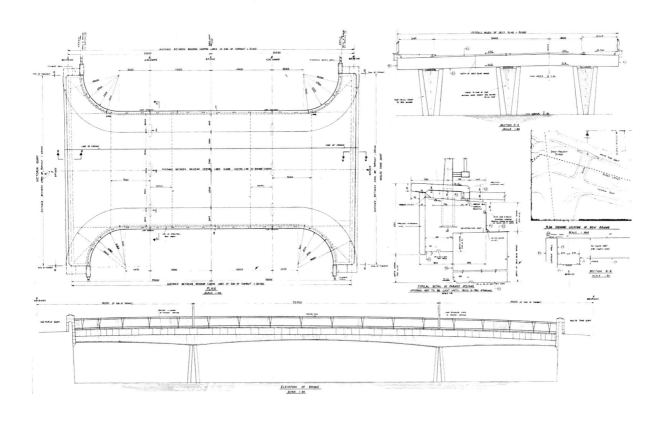

Frank Sherwin Bridge

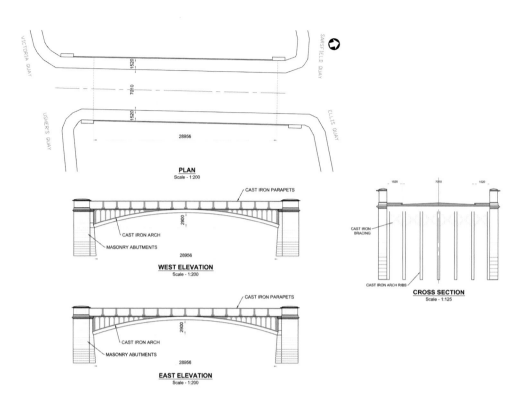

Rory O'More Bridge

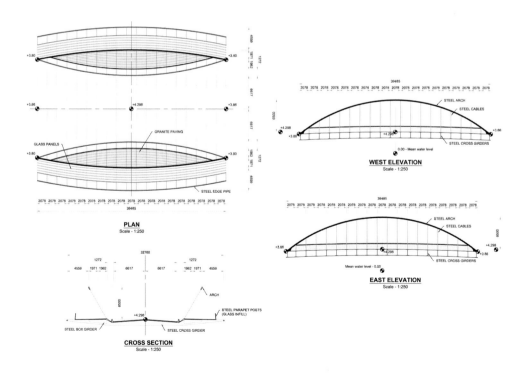

James Joyce Bridge

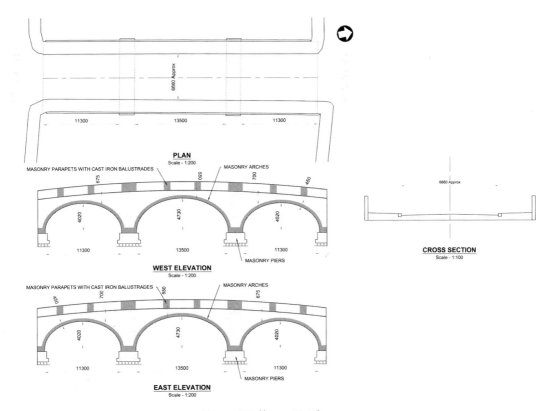

Liam Mellows Bridge

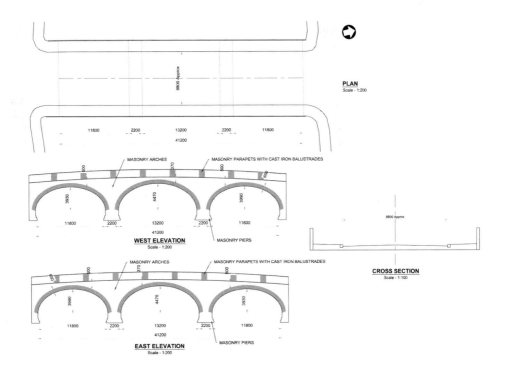

Father Mathew Bridge

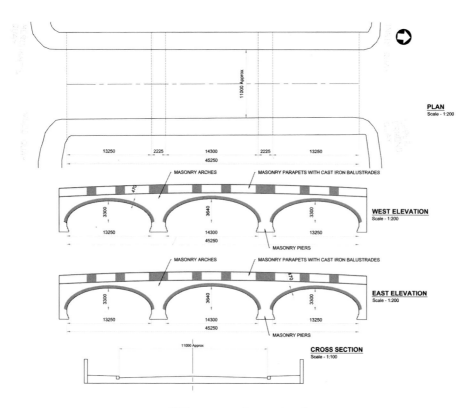

O'Donovan Rossa Bridge

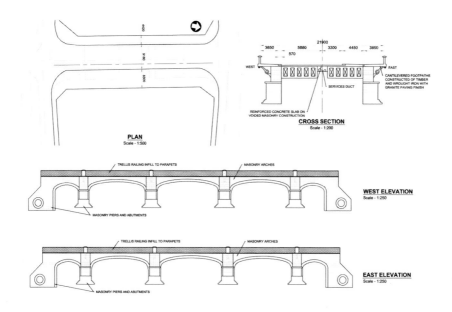

Grattan Bridge

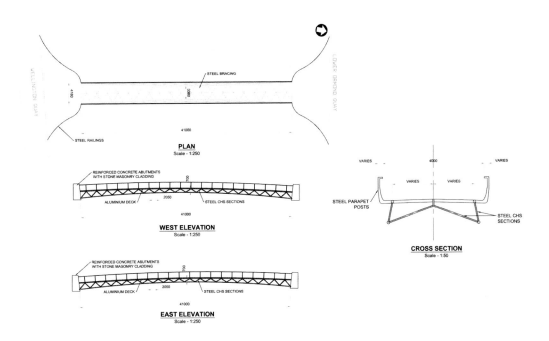

Millennium Bridge

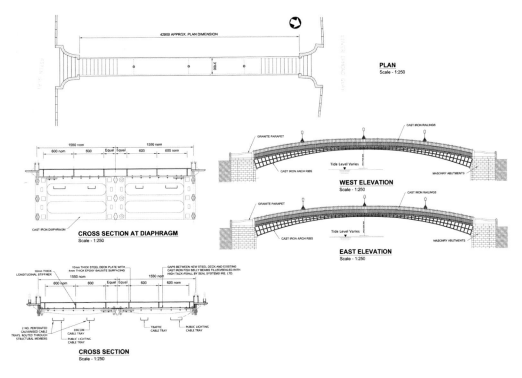

Ha'penny Bridge

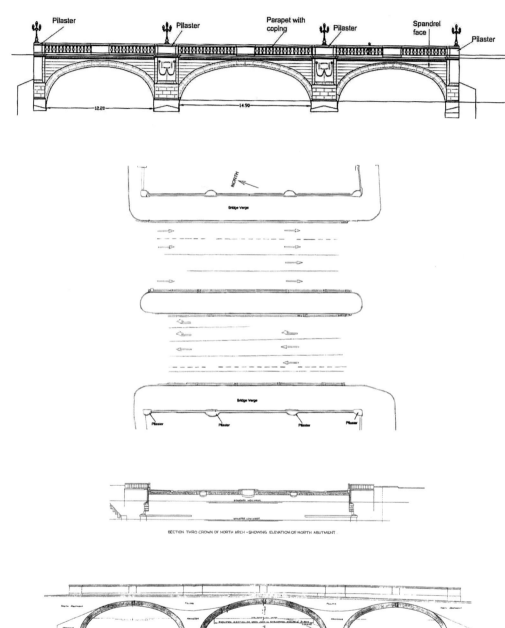

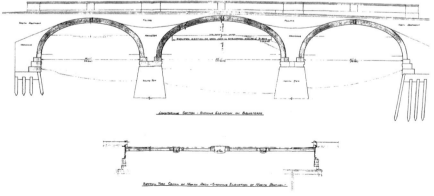

O'Connell Bridge

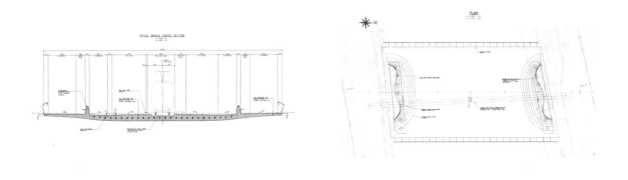

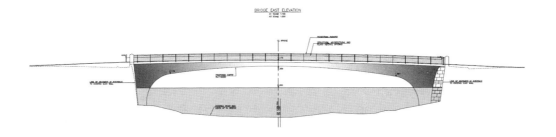

Rosie Hackett Bridge

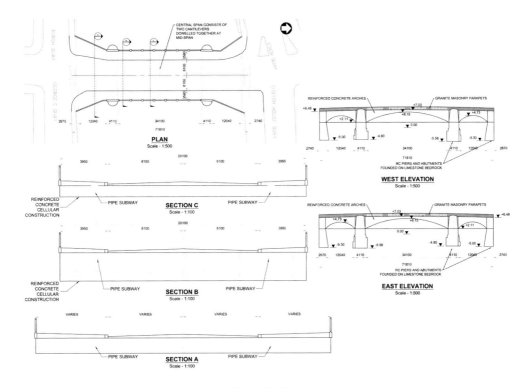

Butt Bridge

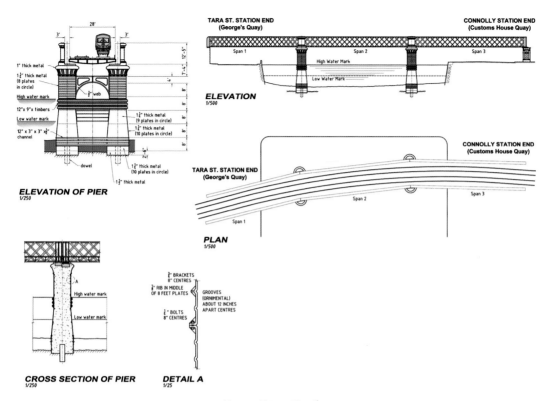

Loop Line Bridge

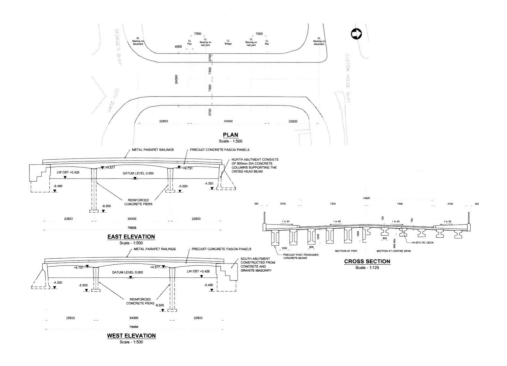

Talbot Memorial Bridge

CROSS SECTION
Scale - 1:250

PLAN
Scale - 1:500

4500

9000

101178

6595   21997   21997   21997   21997   6595

CITY QUAY

CUSTOM HOUSE QUAY

ALUMINIUM DECK WITH
TEXTURED NON-SLIP FINISH

EAST ELEVATION
Scale - 1:500

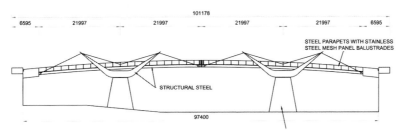

101178

6595   21997   21997   21997   21997   6595

STEEL PARAPETS WITH STAINLESS
STEEL MESH PANEL BALUSTRADES

STRUCTURAL STEEL

97400

Seán O'Casey Bridge

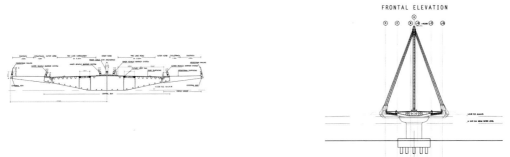

FRONTAL ELEVATION

LONGITUDINAL SECTION

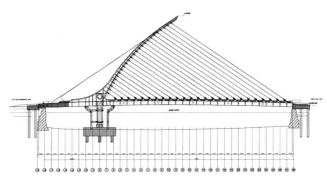

Samuel Beckett Bridge

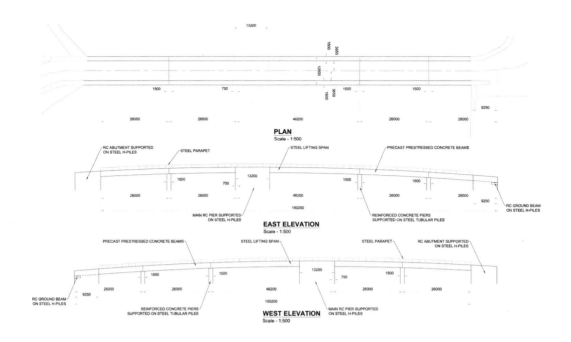

PLAN
Scale - 1:500

EAST ELEVATION
Scale - 1:500

RC ABUTMENT SUPPORTED ON STEEL H-PILES

STEEL PARAPET

STEEL LIFTING SPAN

PRECAST PRESTRESSED CONCRETE BEAMS

MAIN RC PIER SUPPORTED ON STEEL H-PILES

REINFORCED CONCRETE PIERS SUPPORTED ON STEEL TUBULAR PILES

RC GROUND BEAM ON STEEL H-PILES

WEST ELEVATION
Scale - 1:500

PRECAST PRESTRESSED CONCRETE BEAMS

STEEL LIFTING SPAN

STEEL PARAPET

RC ABUTMENT SUPPORTED ON STEEL H-PILES

RC GROUND BEAM ON STEEL H-PILES

REINFORCED CONCRETE PIERS SUPPORTED ON STEEL TUBULAR PILES

MAIN RC PIER SUPPORTED ON STEEL H-PILES

CROSS SECTION AT LIFTING SPAN
Scale - 1:50

STEEL DECK PLATE

TRAPEZOIDAL STEEL STIFFENERS

PRIMARY STEEL GIRDER

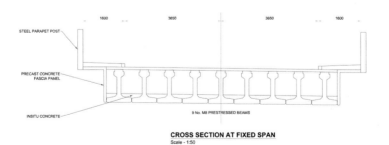

CROSS SECTION AT FIXED SPAN
Scale - 1:50

STEEL PARAPET POST

PRECAST CONCRETE FASCIA PANEL

INSITU CONCRETE

9 No. M8 PRESTRESSED BEAMS

East-Link Bridge

OTHER LIFFEY BRIDGES

The following is a list of the other bridges over the Liffey, from the source in the Wicklow Mountains to Leixlip, just before the Lucan Bridge:

Liffey Head Bridge
Unnamed bridge (below Kippure Mountain)
Ballysmuttan Bridge
Ballyward Bridge
Blessington Bridge (Pollaphuca Reservoir)
Baltyboys Bridge (Pollaphuca Reservoir)
Valleymount Bridge (Pollaphuca Reservoir)
Pollaphuca Bridge
Ballymore Bridge
Old Bridge (Harristown/Brannockstown)
New Bridge (Cramersvalley)
Kilcullen Bridge
Castlemartin Bridge
Unnamed bridge (M9 Motorway/Greenhills)
Unnamed minor bridge (Greenhills)
Athgarvan Bridge
Unnamed bridge
(M7 Motorway/Walshestown/Greatconnell)
Unnamed bridge (Walshestown Cross Roads)
St Conleth's Bridge, (Newbridge Town)
Skeagh Bridge (Yeomanstown)
Victoria Bridge (Yeomanstown/Moortown)
Carragh Bridge (Carragh/Gingerstown)
Railway Bridge Dublin/Cork Line
Leinster Aqueduct
Millicent Bridge
Alexandra Bridge (Clane)
Footbridge K Golf Club
Straffan Bridge
Rock Footbridge (Celbridge Abbey)
Celbridge Footbridge
Celbridge Village Bridge
New Bridge (Parsonstown Reservoir)
Unnamed bridge (M4/Leixlip)
Leixlip Bridge
Bridge at Leixlip Sewerage Treatment Plant

GLOSSARY

Abutment	The ground end-support of a bridge, especially to resist the horizontal thrust of an arch.
Ashlar Masonry	Stone masonry composed of blocks cut to regular size, generally rectangular, laid in courses of uniform height.
Baluster	A short post or pillar in a series supporting a rail or coping and thus forming a balustrade.
Balustrade	A row of balusters topped by a rail, serving as an open parapet, as along the edge of a balcony, terrace, bridge, staircase, or the eaves of a building.
Box girder	A beam with a hollow square or rectangular section.
Cantilever	A beam or member securely fixed at one end and hanging free at the other end.
Capstone	The uppermost or finishing stone of a masonry structure.
Cast Iron	Iron with high carbon content: high compressive strength, low tensile strength.
Cofferdam	A watertight structure allowing underwater foundations to be built in the dry.
Crown:	The highest point of an arch.
Dado	The lower part of a wall marked by a moulding and often of a different surface.
Deck	The floor of a roadway or bridge.
Dublin Corporation	The city government and its administrative organisation in Dublin between 1661 and January 2002, when it was renamed as Dublin City Council.
GS&WR	Great Southern and Western Railway.
Impost	The point where an arch rests on a wall or column, or the upper part of a pier from which an arch springs.
Keystone	The centre or highest voussoir or arch stone.
Lattice	A lattice girder is a type of girder with a criss-crossed web design between the two edges of the girder.
L&NWR	London and North Western Railway.
Masonry	A general term applied to structures made of stone, brick, or concrete.
MGWR	Midland Great Western Railway.
Parapet	A low wall, placed to protect any spot where there is a sudden drop i.e. at the edge of a bridge.
Post-tensioning	This is a technique for reinforcing concrete. Steel strands inside ducts are inserted before the concrete is placed. Afterwards, once the concrete has gained strength the cables are tensioned and anchored. It allows concrete beams and slabs to be thinner.
Pre-stressed concrete	A modern form of reinforcing concrete - tensioned steel strands are embedded in it to impart additional tensile strength.
Soffit	The under-surface of any piece of structure.
Span	Clear distance from face to face of supports.
Spandrel	The space from abutment to abutment in an arch bridge extending from the top of the arch masonry to the top of the roadway.
Springing	The point where the end of an arch meets the abutment.
Steel	An alloy of iron with carbon and other elements, hard, strong and durable. It is used as a structural material. Modern steel-making evolved in the late 19th century.
Truss	A truss bridge is a frame where definite parts are designed to act in tension while other parts act in compression.
Voussoir	A brick or wedge-shaped stone forming one of the units of an arch.
Wrought Iron	Soft and malleable iron with very low carbon content; low compressive strength but high tensile strength. The iron also contains fine fibers of slag. It is easily worked.

INDEX